NORTH OF THE RIVER

North of the River

A brief history of North Fort Worth

J'NELL PATE

with a foreword by Bob Schieffer

TEXAS CHRISTIAN UNIVERSITY PRESS
FORT WORTH

North of the River: A Brief History of North Fort Worth
is number 11 in the Chisholm Trail Series.

Copyright © 1994, J'Nell Pate

Library of Congress Cataloging-in-Publication Data

Pate. J'Nell L.
    North of the river : A brief history of North Fort Worth / by J'Nell Pate
    p. cm.
    Includes bibliographical references and index.
    ISBN 0-87565-133-X (pbk.)
    1. North Fort Worth (Fort Worth, Tex.)— History. 2. Fort Worth
(Tex.)— History. I. Title
F394.F7P375 1994
976.4'5315— dc20

                      94-6502
                       CIP

Cover and text designed by Hal Normand, Shadetree Studio, Fort Worth
Cover photograph by Jim Crocker, Photomedia, Inc., Fort Worth

For Kenneth, always

Contents

Preface

"Cowtown" is not just a label hung on Fort Worth more than a century ago in the heyday of the great cattle drives. Cattle were essential to the city for the entire first century of its existence, and no place embodies that heritage more than the North Side. All that made the city into "Cowtown" took place here — and more. To the North Side came entrepreneurs seeking a fortune and immigrants looking for work, freedom, and security. Their endeavors interlaced to create the most lively, intriguing, complex part of Fort Worth, the place that truly shaped the western image of the city as a whole.

Cowtown began to take shape well before the Civil War, when farm families and livestock breeders from southern states pioneered in North Central Texas, building their homes above the junction of the Clear and West forks of the Trinity River. After the Civil War, the great trail drives came through, bedding down cattle near what is now known as Cold Springs, north of the then-tiny Fort Worth community on the bluff. In 1876, one railroad reached Fort Worth and citizens took full advantage of business opportunities that the rails brought to town.

As the end of the trail drive era loomed, hastened by Kansas's fear of tick-infested Texas cattle and by barbed wire which was slowly strangling the open range, civic leaders worked hard to establish a meat-packing facility on the North Side. Eventually they attracted two major packing houses — Swift and Armour —

to locations in North Fort Worth, which was then incorporated as a separate small city. Early in the twentieth century, those packing houses created work for thousands of people, and immigrants flooded into the community.

In 1909, the City of Fort Worth annexed North Fort Worth, but even today the area retains its distinctive "Cowtown" atmosphere. Tourists and hometown folks alike flock to the Fort Worth Stockyards National Historic District, where rodeo is the sport and where the spirits of the historic cattle industry and the pioneering multi-cultural influences are strong and vibrant in shops, restaurants — well, yes, in bars too — and in the hearts and minds of the people.

People dominate the pages of this story, for as individual people shaped their own destinies, they shaped the character of the city where the West begins — Cowtown — as well. In trying to recreate the history of North Fort Worth, I had to be highly selective. The backgrounds of only a few immigrant families must set the scene and stir the readers' imaginations to visualize the thousands who came to the area. The hard work of the handful of individual, struggling businessmen will have to stand as an example of the hundreds who left lasting, successful legacies to their sons and daughters. The families here described as they attended church, enjoyed an outing in Marine Park, or moved into new homes in Rosen Heights represent all of the close-knit families that made the small city within a city a community.

In one sense, what happened on the North Side was occurring all over America in the first three or four decades of the twentieth century as new communities boomed around one major industry. Americans mingled with the latest arrivals from Europe or Mexico as they moved into small rent houses or even their own newly constructed homes. Because the story took place in Texas, however, and because it began when Fort Worth stood on the western frontier, that which developed north of the Trinity River always will be unique and special to those whose heritage it represents.

Writing a book always requires the help of others. The first person I would like to thank is Richard Selcer who, with Bryan Perkins of Barber's Book Store, suggested the need for several small volumes about the various areas of Fort Worth and their historical significance. Since my dissertation centered on the Fort Worth stockyards (and later was published under the title *Livestock Legacy*), Rick asked me to write a small book on that subject. I proposed a book on the entire North Side of Fort Worth with only a chapter on the stockyards. I thank him for the motivation to get started.

I would like to thank three people — Sue McCafferty, Janie Reid, and Alice Marie Lewis — for the title of this book. For years I've called it my North Side book; then Sue, president of the North Fort Worth Historical Society, suggested "North of the River." I later discovered my friends Alice Marie and the late Janie were tentatively using the same title for their unfinished work on the North Side. Thanks to them for letting me use it.

Thanks to Rita Renfro, Johnny Cabluck, Jenkins Garrett, and Esmond Scarborough for their many suggestions and corrections while reading different stages of my writing. A special thanks to Esmond for lending me various clipping files on the North Side, introducing me to people for interviews, and allowing me to use many of his stories about growing up "north of the river."

I especially thank Bob Schieffer of CBS News for reading the manuscript and graciously consenting to write the foreword. He grew up on the North Side and was a journalism classmate at TCU. Because he is one of the area's most famous sons, I wanted to make certain he was included.

Thanks to Bob Duncan and his late wife Barty for letting me use so many of their postcards of early Fort Worth as photographs. I appreciate all the other folks who let me borrow one or two photographs along the way and those who consented to interviews.

Thanks also to Judy Alter, Tracy Row, and interns Kelli Sheahan, Stacy Dunkel and Ben Gleason of the TCU Press who edited the manuscript and helped me tie up loose ends, state things more precisely, and make sure the facts could be understood clearly.

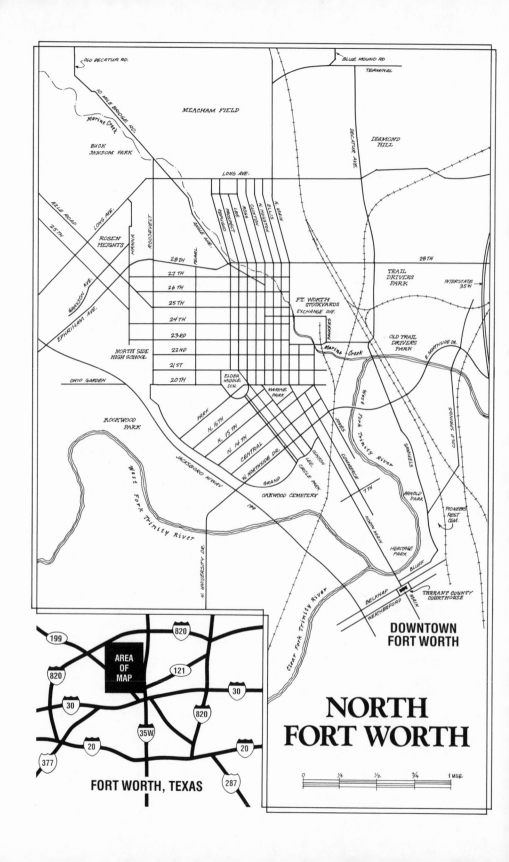

Foreword

by Bob Schieffer

The North Side has always been a special place to me because I grew up in Fort Worth and went to North Side High School. But it was not until years later that I realized how special it was.

As America becomes more homogenized, fewer and fewer of our cities retain individual identities. Atlanta looks a lot like Houston; and franchise row in Rockville, Maryland, looks a lot like franchise row in Buffalo, New York.

Not true of the North Side of Fort Worth which will never be mistaken for another place or even another part of Fort Worth.

Novelist Leonard Sanders once called Fort Worth the "Texasmost City." The North Side has always been its Texasmost part. To be sure, Texas no longer fits the stereotype that many outsiders hold. More urban now than rural, the majority of the state's population is clustered in large cities. But in an age when it is possible for visitors to jet into many parts of the state and never see a cowboy, the North Side is a place where visitors can still rub elbows with a rancher, belly up to a bar where the stools are made of saddles, and, until recently, watch a real, live cattle auction every Monday.

Since the days just after the war with Mexico, when a string of military encampments spread across the frontier to protect settlers from the Plains Indians, Fort Worth has been the stepping-off point to the West, the place "where the West begins." Fort Worth has always taken pride in its western heritage, and no part of the city has taken it more seriously than the North Side.

When Walter Cronkite sent me to Texas during the 1976 presidential campaign to do a CBS News story about the changing Texas electorate, it was only natural that I headed for the North Side with a camera crew. I wanted to get pictures of the cattle auction to show how parts of the old Texas still exist side by side with high-tech Texas.

Behind the auction arena, I found cowboys in boots and hats, looking the way cowboys have looked since the days of the old trail drives. But as these cowboys moved steers from one pen to another they were not riding horses: these ranch hands were astride Japanese motorbikes.

J'Nell Pate's history of the North Side brought back memories of that day and others. I remembered, as a child, going with my family to the stores along North Main to pick out the boots and hats that Santa Claus always brought on Christmas.

I was reminded, too, of the many nights we spent at North Side's LaGrave Field, headquarters for the city's minor league baseball team — the Fort Worth Cats. Trying to keep cool during those pre-air conditioned days just after World War II made many baseball fans rabid.

One of many fascinating accounts in this history is the story of how four members of the Cats team were married one summer night on the LaGrave pitcher's mound. The player-grooms all wore their baseball uniforms and spikes; the brides wore the traditional white gowns and veils. I was there and was awestruck when the teammates who served as groomsmen held their bats aloft and formed an arch for the newlyweds to pass under. West Pointers raise their sabres at the academy's military weddings, but they have nothing on the Fort Worth baseball ceremony. We couldn't have been prouder of the Cats or our city.

Minor league baseball faded after air conditioning and television came to Texas, but the North Side is still the best place in Texas to buy a pair of hand tooled cowboy boots, get the proper crease in a cowboy hat, learn to dance the two-step, and eat authentic Mexican food and barbecue.

During one of the early episodes of the TV soap opera, *Dallas*, I noticed that when the characters wanted to have some fun, they often headed to Fort Worth's North Side. That's still a good plan for a visitor who wants to see a side of Texas that is too often missed.

Where else, after all, are you going to find cowboys riding Japanese motorbikes?

1
Pioneers Plow
the Soil

Two covered wagons lumbered slowly across verdant fields of multicolored flowers on a warm June day in 1848; outriders drove extra animals toward a nearby stand of timber. The two families in the small caravan continued two or three miles northward from where two forks of the Trinity River joined to form one large river just below a tall bluff. North of the bluff an oak-studded slope rose gradually from the river bottoms to a small hill.

Two women, a mother and her married daughter, waited anxiously for their men to decide on a permanent spot for them to live. Finally, Seaborn Gilmore and John B. York, the latter the son-in-law of the older man, found a fertile spot that satisfied them as a place to begin a new life on the Texas frontier. A creek running north from the river would provide sufficient water.

The family had set out in early spring from Missouri, traveling only twelve to fifteen miles a day and becoming increasingly tired of the trail. Having children in the wagons, including a year-old baby, meant trying to wash out clothing each evening and drying it overnight or hanging baby clothes from the moving wagon to catch the sun.

The younger mother, wife of twenty-three-year old York, at least had not left her family behind in Missouri. She and her mother considered the timber in the area as the potential cabins which they wanted the men to hurry and build so they could set up housekeeping and restore some stability to their lives.

Six months later, as Christmas approached, the two families felt reasonably "settled-in." But the death of the York's eighteen-month-old son prevented the celebration of a joyous season. The two mourning families buried him in a stand of trees north of their small settlement.[1]

Besides a few families in the eastern part of what later became Tarrant County, only a dozen or so settlers had found the courage to settle west or south of the bluff. The Yorks and Gilmores became the first families to the north of it. They felt a bit safer the next June, when a company of the U.S. Second Dragoons under a twenty-eight-year-old commander, Major Ripley A. Arnold, established an army camp three miles south of the York and Gilmore farms on the bluff overlooking the junction of the Trinity's two forks. Major Arnold had camped even closer to the Yorks and Gilmores at first, when he and his dragoons stopped near some cold springs northeast of the bluff and down on the river for a few days.[2] However, Arnold moved his camp to the bluff to escape the hordes of mosquitoes in the marshy swamps near the river and to have better protection in case of Indian raids.

Major Arnold named the camp after General William Jenkins Worth under whom he had served in the Mexican War. The farm families who were moving into various parts of Tarrant County needed the protection from Indian raids that the military presence could guarantee.

A second son born to the Yorks on July 1, 1849 and named Will, helped the grieving parents and grandparents get over their earlier loss. Will soon gained a playmate when Celia Gilmore, his grandmother, gave birth to a daughter, Martha Ellen, a few months later.

Gilmore and York became active in early law enforcement efforts in Tarrant County. Gilmore served as the first judge shortly after the Texas legislature organized the local county government in 1850, and citizens chose York as county sheriff for several years. Sadly, York died as a result of his sheriff's duties.

After a drought in the spring of 1863, people had to carry water from the Cold Springs north of downtown. Some tried to take more than their share, but York, as sheriff, made them stand in line and limited what they took. When a man named A. Y. Fowler refused to wait his turn, Sheriff York grabbed him and threw him in a mudhole. Four days later, back in Fort Worth, York walked into the law office of civic leader John Peter Smith and found Fowler waiting. Fowler stabbed York twenty-two times and attempted to flee, but York managed to draw his gun and shoot. Both men died. Friends buried York next to his infant son in the small cemetery.[3]

Gilmore took on the added task of caring for his widowed daughter and her family. As county judge, he had few duties and could spend most of his time fishing and hunting. Fortunately, he was an excellent shot for he now had a larger family to support. The prairies and creek bottoms on the north side of the bluff supplied deer, turkey, squirrels, and other game in abundance. Gilmore hunted deer in the old way, stalking them rather than sitting and waiting for one to go by. After his death in December 1867, Tarrant County residents remembered Gilmore as a man of unblemished character, careful deliberation, almost unerring judgment, and firmness.

Years later, his daughter Martha, born north of the bluff, reminisced about pioneer life: "Why, in those days we had to card wool for our dresses. We wove the cloth to make the men's clothes. Needless to say, there was not much of a variety of clothing for either men or women as is common today."[4]

Martha Gilmore and Will York, along with their brothers and sisters and children of other farm families who had arrived in the area, attended school in the early 1850s on the hill now known as Diamond Hill. The fathers and older brothers of several families cooperated to build a log schoolhouse with a dirt floor. They cut openings in the logs for windows and split and smoothed a few long logs to make benches.

Martha remembered the boys in the class as lively and fun-loving. One of their first teachers was an old, absent-minded fellow who smoked a corncob pipe. He had an unconscious habit of sticking the lighted pipe back in his coat pocket and setting fire to his clothing. One of the older students, Bud Daggett, decided to play a trick on him. Getting some decayed and rotten wood which burned slowly when ignited, Bud slipped a lighted piece in the teacher's pocket as the man passed his desk. The teacher's coat soon caught on fire, much to his excitement. Bud pulled this prank three times in the same day, but the old man never did catch on.[5]

In 1872, Martha Gilmore married Charles Mitchell, the son of a family who had settled on the land which included the small cemetery where the York child and later his father were buried. Charles' mother loved music so much that she had insisted that her piano be moved to Texas with her in a wagon. Eventually, she taught music lessons to youngsters in the area. Parties at the Mitchell house generally included music and always seemed more fun because of the piano. Culture had arrived in the small community.[6]

Other families related by marriage also moved to the area shortly after the Yorks and Gilmores. Two young men who had married sisters back in Tennessee arrived in 1853 in covered wagons. Jack Durrett settled in the valley east of the bluff, and Alfred Johnson settled on what is now Cold Springs Road, east of the present Pioneer's Rest Cemetery. The naturally cold spring near the Johnson farm, about two miles northeast of the present-day courthouse, became a popular watering place for travelers and served as Fort Worth's first water supply. It provided a community gathering place to discuss current events, hear political speakers, and exchange local gossip.[7]

The Johnsons built a log house and extended their hospitality to all newcomers, writing to encourage friends back in Tennessee to emigrate to Texas. Upon hearing that some of their friends had actually decided to come, Mrs. Johnson wrote back quickly with suggestions: "Bring some luxuries and conveniences such as dishes, cooking utensils, mirrors, clocks, bedding, extra clothes. These things are scarce on the frontier."[8]

Ten families joined together to make the trek, all arriving at the Johnson cabin in mid-December. The hosts were ready; they served the newcomers their first Fort Worth meal of fresh venison and a variety of other wild game, plus vegetables they had picked from their garden. The scene resembled a camp meeting with wagons parked around the cabin, their occupants lounging around them, and women spreading bedding under oak and pecan trees for the youngsters to take naps. Then the women began rummaging in their wagons to show the things they had brought. Someone among the newcomers contributed sugar to the meal; the Johnsons had run out quite some time before.[9]

About sundown, after the large meal and its cleanup, Alfred Johnson drove a wagon to the town on the bluff — Fort Worth — to invite several ladies out to the welcoming gathering. A lively conversation flourished among the women over the latest styles and other news from the East. The pioneers from Tennessee even loaned the local ladies a couple of books they had brought with them. The Fort Worth women, hungry for reading material, later took turns with the two recent bestsellers, *Uncle Tom's Cabin* by Harriet Beecher Stowe and *The Scarlet Letter* by Nathaniel Hawthorne. In turn, the local women tried to prepare the recent arrivals for life in a frontier community, telling of the scarcity of staple goods and the effects of the climate and the hard work on clothes and complexions.

Jack Durrett got out his violin and played lively tunes for the gathering. He would be a fixture at weddings and dances for many years.[10]

A large cottonwood tree stood out among the grove of pecan trees that extended to the west from the cold springs. The shade of the huge cottonwood formed a perfect gathering spot for picnics of settlers up on the bluff and nearby farmers on the North Side.[11] The 1857 Fourth of July picnic was a special occasion at the Cold Springs meeting ground. That year, Hardin R. Runnels, a distinguished jurist running for governor, planned to debate his opponent, former U.S. Senator and former president of Texas, General Sam Houston.[12]

The picnic featured a barbecue, and people from all over Tarrant County attended. Colonel Nathaniel Terry, who owned a plantation at the north end of what is now Samuels Avenue, headed the arrangements committee.[13] He made sure that a wagonload of watermelons cooled in the spring all night before the picnic. Next morning he arose early to oversee his slaves as they began cooking pork, beef, and chicken. The feast was set out on tables made out of lumber. Local women helped prepare huge containers of coffee to serve with the pies and cakes they brought.

General Houston was a guest at Colonel Terry's home, while

Runnels stayed with Colonel Middleton Tate Johnson.[14] Colonel Terry and Colonel Johnson each introduced their candidates before their speeches. Afterwards, there was a grand tournament in which riders sped along on horseback with a baton and lifted rings off poles along a quarter mile track.[15]

Even though there were happy occasions such as this July 4th picnic, in June 1871 these pioneer families experienced an unwelcome reminder that they lived on the frontier. A bloody Indian battle took place on Marine Creek, one of the creeks running into the Trinity River.[16] Comanche Indians quietly arrived in the area and began to raid the horse corrals belonging to residents on the north and west edge of the bluff above the Trinity. The Indians drove their stolen horses into some trees along the creek, just east of where present North Main Street and Exchange Avenue intersect. Apparently the Comanches planned to hide in the trees until nightfall. When a white settler who saw the Indians slip into the small wooded area gave the alarm, a posse gathered immediately and surprised the Indians in the thicket. A battle for the horse herd ensued.

Bud Daggett, son of one of the farm families and a former schoolmate of Martha Gilmore, took part in the exchange. "A memorable fight took place," he said. "I personally pulled twenty-seven arrows out of horses in the field."[17]

Several white men died, and the Comanches also killed a large number of the horses. Bud and others of the posse trailed the Comanches due west of the bluff through an area that is now Rockwood Park, but the Indians escaped. Daggett and the other members of the posse never knew how many Comanches they killed or wounded. When they later learned that a band of Indians killed an old woman near White Settlement, they assumed that it was the same party.

Unfortunately, the soldiers in the fort on the bluff had moved away in 1853. The military judged that the frontier had progressed farther west and that Tarrant County settlers no longer needed the troopers. When the Marine Creek raid occurred, the nearest post was Fort Richardson at Jacksboro, sixty miles away.

The early families living north of the Trinity had to visit the little community on the bluff for supplies. A road meandered down the side of the bluff past a few humble cottages to a dead end at the foot of the hill. There a ferry crossed at the confluence of the Trinity's Clear and West forks. If settlers did not want to wait for the ferry, and the river was low, they could cross on horseback or wagon at any one of several fords. When rains made the stream unfordable, the ferry paid for its upkeep several times over.[18]

One of the fords which provided a place to cross the Trinity farther northeast was called Daggett's Crossing. Named in honor of the Charles B. Daggett family who lived nearby and operated a ferry at that spot in the 1850s and 1860s, it was located two and one-half miles northeast of the town on the bluff. Later an east-west bridge, the present Samuels Avenue Bridge, crossed the river there. The Daggett farm covered the area of the present Mount Olivet Cemetery on Twenty-eighth Street.[19]

Eventually citizens constructed a north-south wire suspension bridge across the Trinity River just below the bluff, thus forming the first permanent link between Fort Worth proper and the farming settlements on the North Side. They called the lowlands of the Trinity in that area Battercake Flats, probably because the topography was as flat as a pancake.[20]

Martha Gilmore Mitchell recalled many years later that the men from the North Side enjoyed a favorite meeting place where they whiled away their time during family shopping excursions to Fort Worth. In a one-room ramshackle tavern that stood at an angle on the hillside north of the bluff, they played poker and dominoes for hours, sipping a few "spirits" at the same time. Once the women became so exasperated at their men that they gathered on the south side of the small building, persuaded some of their older sons to help, and shoved the shack down the hill toward the Trinity with the men still inside.[21]

The William Palmer family moved into the neighborhood north of the Trinity in January 1878. Palmer, a Virginian who had fought in the Civil War, took a train west on doctor's orders to look for a more healthful place to live. A malaria sufferer, Palmer chose Tarrant County because of its dry climate and purchased a farm from Charlie Mitchell.

Palmer sent for his property, which arrived later in several rail-

This iron bridge spanned the Trinity River and replaced the original suspension bridge. It pre-dated the Paddock Viaduct which was built in 1913 (North Fort Worth Historical Society).

road cars. Included were the usual furniture and farming implements, but he also had shipped a team of mules, a couple of horses, several head of Durham cattle, a flock of chickens, and three head of bronze turkeys — altogether a veritable rolling ark.[22]

Palmer's fifteen-year-old daughter Laura Alice did not reach Fort Worth until July of that year, when her eastern boarding school term ended. The day after her arrival the family welcomed her with a Fourth of July picnic at "Blue Mound," a scenic spot just a few miles north of their farm.

Laura Alice had only been in her new home two weeks when the Daggetts gave a big dance commemorating the eighteenth birthday of their daughter Tenie. About one hundred young people attended the party, including Laura Alice and her two brothers, Sam and Lan. She did not know the square dances and had never been to a big party like that before, but she was thrilled to get to watch. At midnight the Daggetts called their guests into the dining room to eat from the tables loaded with hams, chicken, pickles, cakes, pies, and much more.

Laura Alice's youth and beauty soon attracted the attentions of many young men, among them Tenie's brother, Bud Daggett, even though he was thirteen years older than she. Bud, long out of school, was raising cattle in the pastures of the North Side. Although she did not know it, Laura Alice had met her future husband.

"E. M. Daggett, Jr. requests the honor of escorting Miss Alice Palmer to church, Sunday Morning July — , 1878."[23] Laura Alice received this note from Bud Daggett a few days after the dance, delivered by eleven-year-old Charles Daggett, Bud's younger brother. After church, Bud stayed to dinner with the Palmer family and spent the afternoon.[24]

Many Sunday dinners later, Bud proposed and Laura Alice accepted. She did not go back to boarding school in Kentucky as her family had planned. Her father insisted that she not marry until she was sixteen, however, so the young couple remained engaged for about a year. Bud began calling her Laura, although her family had always called her Alice.

On her wedding day Laura gained insight into what life with Bud Daggett might be like. She and her parents and friends waited anxiously for Bud to appear so the ceremony could begin. The time came, but Bud still had not arrived. More and more time elapsed. Had her cowboy groom gotten cold feet? Had he been injured or killed in an accident out on the prairie? Bud finally arrived with the explanation that he had been delivering a herd of cattle he had sold that morning. Laura's anger melted away in relief and the ceremony went ahead as planned. The time Bud spent with cattle was something to which Laura became quite accustomed in her life as Mrs. Bud Daggett.[25]

When William Palmer, Laura's father, moved to Missouri in 1887, he sold his farm to Bud and Laura, allowing the young couple to move into the two-story house on the land. Only a year or so later, however, a strong-willed Laura informed Bud that she wanted to move to town. In fact, she would visit her father in Missouri with the children until he decided to move! Bud bought a house at 617 East Weatherford up on the bluff. By then the family consisted of three daughters and a son named Charlie, so Laura no doubt wanted her children to be close to school and church. To lure Laura back to the country, Bud bought a part of the York farm which was south of their own land and built a $10,000 house on it. He moved Laura and the children to the fine new house north of town, but they did not live there very long. In 1891, Bud bought the Tidball place at 607 East Bluff Street in downtown Fort Worth, and there his family remained for many years.

In the 1890s, Bud Daggett suffered financial reverses due to a severe drought. Forced to mortgage his land in order to borrow enough money to feed his cattle, he eventually lost everything except the house on East Bluff Street. To support his family, he secured a job at the newly constructed stockyards on the North Side, working for the North Texas Live Stock Commission Company at $100 per month. Laura took in boarders at their home to help make ends meet. In 1904, Daggett ran for sheriff of Tarrant County, and many stockyards people worked for his election. He lost despite their efforts.[26]

In 1909, Daggett started the Daggett-Keen Commission Company with A. M. Keen. They represented cattlemen in the sale of animals at the stockyards, keeping a small percentage of the price as a commission for their services. Eventually their sons, Charlie Daggett and Clarence Keen, followed their fathers into the business.[27]

Farmers and cattle traders like Bud Daggett were not the only inhabitants of the area north of the bluff after the late 1880s. Fort Worth businessmen became interested in establishing a stockyards and meat packing establishment there. In addition, in 1888 a group of Fort Worth businessmen, operating under the name of Fort Worth City Company, bought approximately 2500 acres extending north from the confluence of the West and Clear forks of the Trinity River to the vicinity of present-day North Twentieth Street. They hired a landscape architect from New York, Nathan Barrett, to lay out the new district. Barrett drew an elaborate street plan for Circle Park, Grand Avenue, and North

Main Street extending north from the courthouse. The developers wanted to connect their new district to the downtown by a viaduct and an electric street railway.[28]

Newcomers did not rush to fill the properties Barrett had plat-ted, but by the end of the nineteenth century many streets, sever-al churches, schools, two or three cemeteries, and a growing live-stock market — with stockyards and packing plants — made the North Side an active community. Sometime after 1890, residents made a request for a post office so they would not have to travel into Fort Worth for their mail. The post office opened in the front corner of a grocery store and was officially designated "Marine."[29]

The small settlement north of the bluff became the nucleus for growth, both for the North Side and the city to the south — Fort Worth — which boasted a population of 26,688 at the turn of the century.[30] The 500 settlers in Marine looked with anticipation for the continued growth of their stockyards and livestock market as the twentieth century arrived.

2
Capitalizing on Cattle

M. G. Ellis was one of the earliest persons besides Bud Daggett to capitalize on cattle in North Fort Worth. Because of his accomplishments in the North Side, Ellis has been honored permanently with a street — just one block west of Main — bearing his name. Tens of thousands of people walk this street, but few realize Ellis's tremendous contributions to the area.

Many old-timers called Merida Green Ellis "The Father of North Fort Worth" because of his leadership in the growth of the stockyards and in the development of a housing addition. His land and wealth gave him the means to make these dreams come true, but it was not always so.

Born in Denton County in 1847 of parents who had come from Missouri the year before, Ellis was orphaned as an infant and subsequently raised by his mother's sister and her husband, Mr. and Mrs. Samuel P. Loving. They moved to Tarrant County when Ellis was two. As a young man, Ellis worked as a clerk. Later, after becoming a partner in the Boaz and Ellis firm, he bought out Boaz. By 1876, Ellis had shifted to the booming agricultural supplies and implements business, selling plows on commission. In 1881, however, the doctor ordered Ellis to retire because of his health. Ellis sold his business to his new partner Walter A. Huffman and became a gentleman cattle dealer. He built a house on his 1,067 acres north of Fort Worth, fenced and stocked the land with cattle and horses, and established four dairies.[1]

The one-room Marine Common School accommodated all pupils north of the river in the 1890s. The teacher in 1892 was Lee M. Hammond (North Fort Worth Historical Society).

By 1883, when he moved his family to the area, Ellis saw the necessity for a school. The children needed something better than the old log structure where Martha Gilmore, Will York, and Bud Daggett studied more than two decades earlier. Ellis bought land, and the next year built a one-room frame school which seated twenty students.[2] Miss Carrie Campbell served as the first teacher. Her pupils carried their own drinking water from the spring nearly one-half mile away. At first the boys carried the water during recess or the noon hour, but they soon tired of doing it and let the bucket remain empty. Yet when Miss Campbell let the boys out of class to carry the water, they readily volunteered.[3]

Patrons began calling the new frame school the Marine Common School, and the community due north of the courthouse, Marine, because of Marine Creek which ran southeasterly through the area. G. W. Hewitt opened the first grocery store there in 1889, at the northeast corner of North Main and Central Avenue.[4]

In 1905, community taxpayers rebuilt the school with brick, enlarging it to accommodate all grades. The Fort Worth Public School Board honored Ellis nine years later by renaming the brick

The M. G. Ellis School was built in 1905 at the corner of North
Main and Fourteenth streets (North Fort Worth Historical
Society).

school in his honor. The impressive building served North Side
children for decades, though it had stood vacant for several years
before catching fire in 1986. The building that had helped create
thousands of memories burned to the ground.[5]

Ellis's business interests multiplied, making him hardly a man
in retirement. Not only did he help organize the Fort Worth
Packing Company in 1890, but he also became vice-president of
the Union Stock Yards National Bank in 1889 and operated a
livestock commission business at the stockyards from 1891 to
1893.

Apparently Ellis's health was not as bad as his doctor had led
him to believe; he lived to be eighty-five. At his funeral in 1932
the minister said, "A life so fruitful should not excite grief but

rather rejoicing at its end. . . . Such a life as his must inspire those whom he has left."[6]

~

Before M. G. Ellis encouraged growth and settlement in the North Side and operated his dairies there, cattle drives from South Texas provided the major commercial activity for all of Fort Worth. As a boy, Howard W. Peak, born in Fort Worth in 1856, marveled at the large herds of cattle being driven through his hometown: "I used to watch hundreds of thousands of beef cattle as they passed in enormous herds."[7] Bud Daggett also remembered, "I sometimes saw 30,000 to 40,000 cattle in a single day."[8]

Some say that the very first herd ever to pass through Fort Worth belonged to a Colonel J. J. Meyers of Lockhart, Texas, who trailed his cattle to Sedalia, Missouri, in the spring of 1866.[9] Every year thereafter, cattle arrived in Fort Worth south of downtown, near present-day South Hemphill Street. From there, they turned northeastward through what is now the Texas and Pacific Railroad yards, came north on present Commerce and Jones streets, and passed east of Pioneer's Rest Cemetery. The men and their herds then followed the Cold Springs Road to Daggett's Crossing. There they crossed the Trinity, swung around the hill where Trail Drivers' Park is now located on Twenty-eighth Street, and turned north. Interstate 35 eventually followed what had once been the well-worn northward trail.

The trail crossed the Trinity River about a half mile east of the present stockyards area. Often the sun was sinking low in the west when the herds and their drovers arrived. The cowboys bedded their cattle down in the broad valley below the bluff a day or two before continuing the long drive. The trail hands would travel into Fort Worth to visit the waiting saloons and general stores to drink and purchase the supplies needed for the next hundred-mile leg of the journey.

One of these cattlemen was named Reuben Jenkins, called "Rube" by his friends. He later said he had thought about buying land in the valley but decided that it would never be worth anything.[10]

Drovers then called the trail to Abilene the Texas Trail or the Great Trail. However, in Indian territory, it connected with Jesse Chisholm's old trade route, and eventually people applied the name Chisholm Trail to the entire length of the trail from south of San Antonio to Kansas. Fort Worth became the last stopping point to buy supplies before the herds crossed Indian territory and reached Abilene. Already the community was earning a nickname of "Cowtown."

The transition from a temporary stopover to a large meat-packing center rivaling Kansas City and Chicago took tremendous effort on the part of Fort Worth businessmen. It consumed a third of a century, but they did it. First they had to attract railroads. The Texas and Pacific arrived July 19, 1876.

Meat packing plants and stockyards were the next order of business.[11] After some aborted efforts, local men made a successful start. John Peter Smith, Morgan Jones, and J. W. Burgess obtained a charter on July 26, 1887, to build a stockyards north of the downtown area.[12] The men raised $200,000 in capital and called their new company the Fort Worth Union Stock Yards. Before they could construct the yards and open for business, however, they had to reorganize.

Fifty-year-old Colonel Henry Clay Holloway, whom many would call the "Father of the Fort Worth Stockyards," ceremoniously drove the first stake into the ground as construction began in 1888. When the yards opened for business in July 1889, he became the first manager.[13]

Holloway came to Tarrant County from South Carolina in 1858, at age twenty. He later married Margaret Loving, who was related to the family who had raised M. G. Ellis. After returning from service in the Civil War, Holloway purchased a farm of several hundred acres, adjacent to Ellis's holdings. He made his primary living, however, in a hardware and grocery store in Fort Worth with a partner named W. W. Trippett. The two men benefitted from the trail herds passing through in the 1870s. "No more truthful, enterprising and upright man than Colonel Holloway ever lived," Trippett said after they dissolved their partnership.[14]

The stockyards under Holloway's management covered 258

acres, stretching three-quarters of a mile along the Trinity River. Holloway oversaw the construction of a two-story wooden exchange building and hotel.

While the new livestock facilities were being built, Andrew T. Byers led Fort Worth businessmen in constructing an electric railway from the downtown area to the stockyards. Byers and his associates contracted with a Detroit firm to construct ten-and-a-half miles of track at a cost of $60,000. Their line became the first electric street railway in the entire Southwest in the summer of 1889. Its powerhouse sat near the northern side of an old iron bridge which stood where a ferry once ran, about one-half mile west of the bluff over the Trinity River.[15] Neither the powerhouse nor the iron bridge remain today. The county, city, and railway company shared the expense of building a new metal bridge that would support the railway over the Trinity.

Before the electric rails were built, mules pulled the streetcar up Main Street and if it got overloaded, passengers had to get out so the car could make it up even a slight grade.[16] Yet the 500 horsepower boiler, which provided electricity for the North Side Street Car Company, was "the largest single boiler in any electrical works in the south." It could easily provide enough power for a car carrying twenty passengers.[17]

Soon after the stockyards opened, cattlemen rested and fed cattle there before shipping them north to the Kansas City or St. Louis markets. Cattle drives, except for short distances, were a thing of the past.

Local businessmen, including M. G. Ellis, chartered the Fort Worth Packing Company in April 1890, with a capital stock of $200,000.[18] When the packing plant opened in December of that year, they expected cattlemen to sell their cattle for slaughter in Fort Worth. Unfortunately, most cattlemen preferred to sell their cattle to the larger and busier markets farther north. The Fort Worth packing plant lacked the finances to pay cash immediately for the livestock they purchased, and the cattlemen did not like that. Ellis, Holloway, and the other stockholders, including down-

Above, the first Stockyards Hotel and Exchange Building featured verandas on both stories at the front. The structure was torn down in 1902 and replaced by the current exchange (North Fort Worth Historical Society).

town businessman John Peter Smith, needed money to expand their operation and gain the cattlemen's confidence.

Mike C. Hurley, a Fort Worth railroad contractor, had his own reasons for wanting the Fort Worth market to succeed — railroad expansion. Consequently, he traveled to Boston to try to interest eastern investors in the Fort Worth operation. Texans may have grown the cattle, but the East had the money.

Hurley, an Irishman who had lived in Fort Worth since age twelve with a widowed mother and eight siblings, helped his family in his youth by working for fifty cents a day breaking farmland with oxen. Apparently a fellow with an iron constitution, he later worked in a brickyard and hauled coal for seven cents an hour. At age seventeen in 1868, he began railroad construction work, and in 1885, only in his mid-thirties, he proved that he possessed more than a strong back by organizing his own company: the Fort Worth and New Orleans Railway. His efforts brought the Rock Island Railroad to Fort Worth in 1893. Interested in all aspects of the city, Hurley invested in the Farmers and Mechanics National Bank and helped organize the packing plant on the North Side. When he went to Boston as the spokesman for Fort Worth, he could talk to the eastern money men with authority.[19]

As a result of Hurley's promotion, Greenlief W. Simpson and his lawyer, W. C. Johnson, visited the Fort Worth Union Stock Yards and Fort Worth Packing Company plant in October 1892. Simpson had recently sold the Bay State Cattle Company in Boston, which had provided him considerable experience in the business aspects of slaughtering beef.

When Simpson and Johnson visited the North Side, a railroad washout had stranded several thousand cattle at the yards. Pens with the normal capacity for 150 railroad cars of cattle were forced to hold three times that many.

"This is some market," Simpson noted to his lawyer as he looked at all those cattle in the pens. Whether Hurley, Holloway, and the other investors told the Boston men of the railroad washout is unknown. They probably did not, because Simpson and Johnson, impressed by the sheer magnitude of the market, decided to buy.[20] Simpson and several of his friends first created a new company, chartered in West Virginia because of less restrictive corporate regulations there. They called it the Fort Worth Stock Yards Company. Then they bought the Fort Worth Union Stock Yards and the Fort Worth Packing Company from the local owners. A neighbor of Simpson in Boston, Louville V. Niles, invested as well.[21]

Although Simpson, Niles, and fellow investors poured in money and business expertise, they struggled with their company for nearly a decade. A nationwide panic in 1893 hurt business; so did Texas cattlemen's distrust of outsiders, especially easterners. They still preferred to ship their cattle to Kansas City and St. Louis.

Simpson attended the annual convention of the Cattle Raisers Association of Texas (now the Texas and Southwestern Cattle Raisers Association) and urged cattlemen to ship to Fort Worth.

"You've got a market here, gentlemen," Simpson reminded. He also promised to pay the cattlemen fifty cents per head more than what they could get in Kansas City.[22]

The new stockyards owners also hired a public relations agent, Charles C. French. French had traveled from Pennsylvania to Texas in the late 1870s to join two brothers who already lived in the state. After spending two seasons driving cattle to northern markets, French raised sheep for a while and then got a job as buyer and traveling representative for first one and then another Chicago cattle commission firm. Because he had traveled all over Texas, Arkansas, and Louisiana and knew most of the livestock raisers, French seemed to Simpson and Niles to be the person who could represent the Fort Worth market well.

One day while doing some business in Fort Worth, French encountered Charles McFarland, a cattleman who lived in Weatherford.

"How are things going?" McFarland asked.

"Things are awfully slow at the stockyards. We need something to attract some business at the market," French answered.

"Why not have a fat stock show? That will create some interest," McFarland suggested.

"We're not getting any fat stock in now," French complained.

"I'll bring some of mine to show, and we can probably persuade some of the other ranchers," McFarland said, refusing to drop a good idea.[23]

French went to W. E. Skinner, who replaced Holloway when he had resigned as manager of the stockyards. Skinner liked the idea and presented it to Simpson and Niles. McFarland carried through on his promise to persuade some of his ranching friends to show their cattle; Samuel Burk Burnett, Marion Sansom, J. W. Burgess, and several others agreed to bring their best animals.

The ranchers and the stockyards officials agreed on a date in early March 1896. Excitement prevailed the day before the show as railroad cars of cattle arrived to be unloaded and cowboys herded others from surrounding pastures into the yard. Owners tied their show cattle to trees on Marine Creek just west of the Exchange Building in the stockyards. Promoters waited with anticipation to see if many people would attend.

As happens frequently in Texas in the early spring, a sleet and snowstorm developed overnight. French, McFarland, and the other promoters awoke the next morning to a sense of foreboding as they looked out their windows and found the ground blanketed in white. When they got to the stockyards, they found the animals huddled under the trees, their backs covered with icy whiteness. The men cursed the weather for ruining their grand event.

Later that morning, the sun shone so brightly that the snow blinded cattlemen and stockyards officials as they wandered about the yards. Then the snow and sleet began to melt; by noon, all moisture had evaporated. The show of outstanding stock proceeded as planned.

The stockyards company promoters had constructed a small grandstand for visitors. During the proceedings, one cantankerous steer got loose, headed straight for the wooden grandstand and almost tore it down amidst squealing spectators. Then he charged south out of the stockyards area with two cowboys trying to rope him. They could not swing their lariats because of the brush and limbs of the trees, so the steer got away.[24]

Officials awarded prizes of boots, saddles, buckles, and even a windmill, collected from merchants by French and other promoters. The show turned out to be a success after all, and local cattlemen promised to cooperate for later events.

The stockyards and packing company represented the biggest business on the North Side. Simpson and Niles realized, however, that they needed more than a fat stock show to attract business to their market. Livestock receipts fluctuated, making it difficult for the business to pay farmers and ranchers promptly when thousands of cattle arrived in one day. Niles left his family in Boston and spent about six months each year from 1899 to 1901 living in the Stockyards Hotel, which allowed him personally to oversee the operation of the meat-packing facility adjacent to the stockyards.

The two major stockholders began negotiating with the two largest meat packers in the nation, Armour and Swift, in the spring of 1901. If either of these slaughter-house giants could be persuaded to build a plant on the North Side, the problem would be solved, for each could handle financing the large receipts of livestock promptly.

Armour and Swift both expressed interest in relocating, but they wanted the city of Fort Worth to give them an inducement, the same way cities had given bonuses or lands to railroads a generation earlier. Simpson and Niles owned land at the stockyards, so they agreed to give each packer approximately twenty-one acres on which to build. During the summer of 1901, citizens of Fort Worth started a campaign to raise a $50,000 bonus for each meat-packing company.[25] Simpson and Niles even agreed to reorganize their company and give one-third of it to each of the two meat packers, retaining only one-third for themselves.[26] They reasoned quite logically that owning one-third of a successful company would yield greater profits than owning all of a near-bankrupt business.

Citizens of Fort Worth held a meeting early in October to try to raise the rest of the money needed for the bonus. After a long but successful session, the citizens threw their hats in the air and cheered.[27]

"Fort Worth started on her road to greatness last night," proclaimed a story in the Fort Worth Register the following morning.[28] The final deal made J. Ogden Armour president of the Fort Worth Stock Yards Company, Edward Swift, vice-president, and Simpson, second vice-president.[29]

Simpson gave a keynote address at a ceremony which launched construction on the new facilities. A large crowd assembled at 9 A.M. on January 10, 1902, overflowing the porch of the combination Stockyards Hotel and Exchange Building. Spectators moved out on the front lawn at Simpson's urging.

"Gentlemen, we are entering upon an era that will be beneficial alike to producer, manufacturer and consumer. In order to have this enterprise inaugurated in a practical way we have invited Colonel H. C. Holloway, who has been identified with all the phases of the stockyards and packing house progress in Fort Worth, to cut the tree whose removal is necessary to carrying out the great plans we have in view."[30]

One of the large trees that had provided the setting for that first snowy stock show in 1896 stood in the way of the expansion which Armour and Swift intended. But before striking the tree, Colonel Holloway reminisced about the businessmen of Fort

Worth who had begun the first stockyards on the same spot over a decade earlier. Holloway had driven the first stake in the ground at that time too. The Colonel then stepped over to the doomed oak tree and accepted the axe with which to strike the first blow for a brighter future for Fort Worth.

Each of the important dignitaries in the crowd took a symbolic swing at the tree as the rest of the people cheered. M. G. Ellis participated, as did E. M. Daggett (Bud Daggett's uncle.) Ten minutes elapsed before the tree finally fell.

Celebrations honoring the new facilities apparently continued all year. The management of the Stock Yards Inn even arranged for a hot-air balloon to rise in a blaze of fireworks at dusk on August 22 in front of their hotel. A man who billed himself as "Professor Haley" announced that he would ascend to a height of 5,000 feet in a thirty-eight-foot-diameter balloon and then leap from the basket to the ground in a parachute. The promoters expected a crowd of several thousand and took out advertisements in the newspapers several days in advance, urging the public to take the streetcars early to avoid the rush. Since no record of Haley's feat appeared in the newspapers after the big day, it can only be assumed that the professor was successful as Fort Worth's first professional "sky diver."[31]

The newly reorganized stockyards company kept the air filled with the sounds of construction. Workers tore down the old Exchange Building of the Fort Worth Union Stock Yards and in 1903 completed the large, two-story stucco Spanish-style Livestock Exchange Building that still stands. The packing plants opened on March 4, 1903, during the annual fat stock show. As evidence of the importance of all the new construction in the area, North Main Street was the only street north of downtown Fort Worth that was paved.[32]

Stockyards officials invited "everybody" to an open house at the yards, "especially the ladies." Planners of the event even invited the governor and all the state legislators, but they were in session in Austin and did not come.[33]

Both Armour and Swift held open house at their meat-packing plants from 9 A.M. to 5 P.M. on March 5, 6, and 7, 1903. Tour guides explained each step in the slaughtering process. Drizzling

*Above, the Fort Worth Stockyards Company Livestock Exchange,
about 1920, with the Armour & Company plant in the background. The Swift and Company plant is pictured below. The
building in the foreground, originally local headquarters, serves as
a restaurant today (both photos courtesy of the North Fort Worth
Historical Society).*

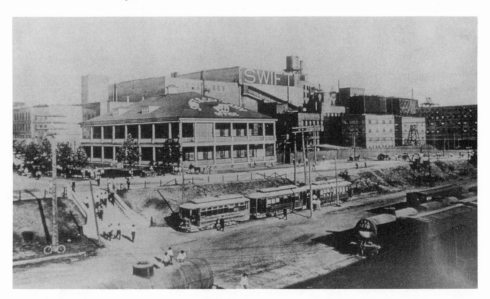

rain and slush underfoot did not prevent a large crowd from assembling for the festivities. Various commission companies doing business at the stockyards and packing plants gave out hundreds of dollars worth of free badges, calendars, buttons, and pencils to visitors during the grand opening and the fat stock show.[34]

In November 1903, when the National Live Stock Exchange held a convention at the Worth Hotel, local livestock interests showed the visitors around the new exchange building.[35] Clearly, big business had arrived in Fort Worth. The Fort Worth Stock Yards Company owned the Reporter Publishing Company, the Fort Worth Belt Railway Company, the Stockyards National Bank of North Fort Worth, the Fort Worth Cattle Loan Company, and the North Fort Worth Townsite Company — in other words, just about everything that was connected with the livestock market on the North Side.

A young man named Joseph Googins arrived in Fort Worth in 1902 as a Swift employee to administer many of these businesses for the absentee packing-plant owners. Born in Chicago, the twenty-eight-year-old Googins grew up in the shadow of the Union Stock Yards there. He came to Texas for his health at age twenty and worked as a cowboy on several ranches in South Texas before returning to Chicago a few months later. He was hired by the Chicago Provision Company, which had bought out the struggling Fort Worth Packing Company, and was sent to Fort Worth in the 1890s as a livestock buyer. He stayed only a year before returning to Chicago, where he accepted a job as a livestock buyer for Swift and Company.

His background in the cattle business gave Googins the experience Swift thought necessary to send him back to Fort Worth as their representative in the North Fort Worth Townsite Company. Googins's goal was to develop North Fort Worth. This followed a pattern that meat packers often pursued in communities where they established plants: to buy up land around the yards and wait for the value to increase. The railroads had used the same approach a generation earlier, though they obtained government land free.

In 1904, Googins began managing Swift's entire plant in Fort Worth in addition to their interests in the stockyards and the townsite company. He also served on the board of directors of the fat stock show and the Chamber of Commerce. Fort Worth eventually became Googins's permanent home. Many years later, his daughter Ruth married Elliot Roosevelt, son of President Franklin D. Roosevelt. This family connection brought Eleanor Roosevelt and other members of the Roosevelt clan to Fort Worth for numerous visits over the years. Promoters never failed to reserve a prominent box seat for any Roosevelts when they came to town during the annual fat stock show.[36]

Just as Simpson and Niles had hoped, after Armour and Swift opened their plants in 1903, the cattlemen of Texas began trusting the financial status of the Fort Worth market. As a consequence, receipts increased dramatically. Boom times arrived on the North Side. Within a year, twelve commission companies handled business for the cattlemen, and these companies kept increasing in number.

Fort Worth ranked as the nation's fifth largest livestock market by 1904 and by the end of the decade stood third behind only Chicago and Kansas City. The market vacillated between third and fourth place for the next fifty years. It always ranked as the largest market south of Kansas City and the largest in the entire Southwest during that half century.[37]

Meanwhile, people began flocking to the North Side in search of jobs. Immediately after arriving in the city, by rail or otherwise, these newcomers caught a streetcar up North Main Street to Exchange Avenue, got a job, and then usually settled nearby. Labor needs of the stockyards and the Swift and Armour plants soon swelled the population from 500 to 5,000.

The meat packing plants proved to be a place where a young man could start out at the bottom and work his way up to a position of importance in thirty or forty years. Kenneth Neidholt began as a butcher and ended in the superintendent's office after forty years at Armour and Company.[38] J. E. Cavender began as a clerk in Swift's mailing department at age seventeen. In forty-six and one-half years he missed only six days of work, three of those

playing baseball for the Swift team, and eventually became superintendent of the refinery section.[39]

Frances Young was a teenager just out of North Side High
School in 1933 when she started work at Swift for $12 a week.
She worked in the credit department until she retired in 1971
when the plant closed.[40]

Swift and Company provided medical care, emergency leave,
and a pension plan. Other fringe benefits included company picnics, a band, a baseball team, bridge clubs, and educational classes
for workers.[41] Armour and Company provided many of the same
benefits.

Since most of the workers lived near the two large packing
plants, a real sense of community developed on the North Side.
Many Swift management officials lived on Grand Avenue.[42]

~

With the outbreak of World War I in Europe, boom times
arrived at the stockyards. So many foreign governments bought
cavalry animals in the city that the North Side market center
became the largest horse and mule market in the world. In one
eight-month period from the end of November 1914 through July
1915 allied governments spent more than five million dollars in
Fort Worth for horses and mules. During 1917, the year the
United States entered World War I, the Fort Worth market also
broke all previous records of animal receipts, reaching totals that
were not surpassed until World War II. Over three and one-half
million animals of all types — cattle, calves, hogs, sheep, horses
and mules — arrived at the yards in that one year.[43] For the first
time, defense spending was pouring money into the Fort Worth
economy. In future years, in one form or another, defense expendi-
tures would become a permanent and significant element in the
city's financial climate.[44]

Waddy R. Ross was one man who benefitted from the war-relat-
ed boom. He and his brothers Sam and R. E. owned one of the
largest horse and mule dealerships: the Ross Brothers Horse and
Mule Company, housed in the new horse and mule barns at the
stockyards. With his World War I business profits, Waddy Ross

Four representatives of the Ross Brothers Horse and Mule dealers of Mule Alley show off their wares (North Fort Worth Historical Society).

constructed a 6,000-square-foot, fifteen-room, two-and-one-half story brick house on the corner of Grand Avenue and Park Street in 1917. Ross, a self-made millionaire, was one of the founders and supporters of the fat stock show.[45]

Stockyards livestock receipts boomed again when World War II began in Europe and the need for food increased. Efforts of Texans to promote sheep production succeeded admirably in the late 1930s so that by the 1940s producers were able to market two million sheep each year at Fort Worth. Ironically, during the war years, "Cowtown" ranked as the largest sheep market, not just in the nation, but in the world. The year 1944 brought the largest receipts ever at Fort Worth — 5.25 million animals of all types — cattle, calves, sheep, hogs, horses, and mules.[46] As producers brought their animals to the Fort Worth market, they made Exchange Avenue the busiest short street in town. The hotels stayed full, the bars blared forth noisy and rowdy music, and live- stock producers from all over Texas made their way to businesses on either Main or Exchange to spend their money.

By the height of World War II, forty-eight commission compa- nies operated on the yards selling cattle for Texas livestock pro- ducers. Nearly 7,000 workers from all over Fort Worth earned their livelihood directly from one of the enterprises at the stock- yards, continuing to make the livestock industry the largest single employer in Fort Worth, as it had been for half a century. Many workers awoke at 5:30 A.M. when the Swift whistle blew and made their way to Swift's or Armour's packing plant. Others were employed by the Fort Worth Stockyards Company itself. These men put out hay, checked the water in the pens, and drove stock down the alleys to the weighing scales for the commission agents or traders. They also unloaded cattle, sheep, or hogs from railroad cars that continuously moved in and out of the yards.

During peak periods, 500 railroad carloads of livestock might be in pens awaiting sale. Unfamiliar with their crowded surround- ings, the cattle, sheep, hogs, horses, and mules added their bawl- ing, bleating, squealing, or neighing to the distinctive cacophony. The constant din of frightened animals became so familiar to stockyards workers that they learned to tune it out and go on with unloading or caring for the animals. Cursing cowboys, determined livestock owners, or wheeling-dealing independent traders added to the noisy atmosphere as they wandered from pen to pen, crowded the alleys, or gathered in the Exchange Building.

Residents within a three-mile radius lived with the constant sounds and smells of the yards. They too became so accustomed to the noise that it lulled them to sleep at night. The smell of the stockyards as it wafted through the night air brought a reassurance of sorts to the families that they belonged to a community, that their livelihoods were secure, that they had a purpose for each day. The 5:30 A.M. whistle at Swift and Company belonged to all of them.

A view of the stockyards at the height of activity — the 1940s.
The coliseum, exchange building, and horse and mule barns are
surrounded by cattle pens (Texas and Southwestern Cattle Raisers
Foundation).

During those booming, bustling war years, workers on the
North Side helped feed the people of two continents. Armour and
Swift extended shifts, and stockyards activity never ceased. By the
time the war ended in the summer of 1945, however, changes
began that would alter many lives. Government restrictions limited the hours in which buying and selling could occur at the yards.
Railroad shipments declined because country markets had opened
up in small towns during the war. Farmer's new pick-up trucks purchased with high wartime livestock prices carried animals to local
small town auctions rather than to Fort Worth.

While these marketing changes happened far from Fort Worth,

local factors also contributed to a decline in the North Side's major industry. By the end of the 1940s, aircraft manufacturers employed more people than the livestock industry, and the numbers of livestock workers and receipts began a gradual decline. The reign of the stockyards over the Fort Worth economy was gradually coming to an end.

Receipts at the Fort Worth Stockyards fell to two million animals per year in the 1950s but remained constant at that figure for the entire decade. The steady business was due in part to massive publicity by the local livestock interests in an effort to keep their market strong. Yet at the end of the decade, a new phenomenon in livestock marketing emerged which challenged the large terminal markets again. In these "feed lots," thousands of cattle remained in pens in the heart of the grain country — Lubbock, Amarillo, western Kansas — to be fed the corn and grain necessary to provide choice cuts of beef demanded by restaurants and supermarkets.

From the two million animals at the beginning of the 1960s to one million by mid-decade, Fort Worth Stockyards receipts dropped to only 500,000 by 1971.[47] The end for Armour in Fort Worth had already come, however. Declining numbers of animals for slaughter and an outdated plant were symptomatic of the problems facing the meat-packing industry. Adding to the woes, the meat packer could not compete with lower wages paid by small independent companies; when Armour asked the CIO-affiliated butchers' union to take a wage cut to keep the operation going, the union refused. Armour closed its doors in 1962.

In contrast, the independent National Brotherhood of Packing House Workers Union at Swift (created in 1937 when the Wagner Act banned company unions) negotiated to accept wage cuts in order to keep their plant operating. Consequently, Swift and Company remained open until 1971.[48]

With the two plants closed, many residents of the North Side lost jobs. Older persons ready to retire did so, but others had to seek jobs elsewhere. Unemployment in the North Side became a severe problem among the new wave of less educated immigrants, many of whom were from Mexico.

By the mid-1980s, barely 100,000 cattle arrived each year,

fewer than the number of longhorns driven through Fort Worth when the cattle drives were at their peak at the end of the 1860s. Only a trickle appeared at the Monday-only sales by the early 1990s. The market held its last auction December 21, 1992. Fort Worth now wears the proud title of "Cowtown" because of past glory in the livestock marketing field, not as a continuing accomplishment.

In honor of businessmen who had capitalized on the millions of cattle that came through the North Side and the earliest cowboys who trailed the herds northward, city leaders dedicated Trail Drivers' Park just off Twenty-eighth Street, northeast of the stockyards. When the City of Fort Worth purchased thirty-seven acres of land for a park in 1928, George W. Saunders of San Antonio, president of the Old Trail Drivers Association, wrote to the Fort Worth Board of Park Commissioners suggesting that the park they were contemplating in Diamond Hill be named "Trail Drivers' Park" to commemorate the trail herds and their drivers who bedded down in the area on their way north to Abilene. Saunders estimated that sixty percent of the ten million cattle driven to northern markets in those early days came through Fort Worth. He had driven many of them himself.

A Diamond Hill Civic League, organized in 1925, also urged the city to create the thirty-seven-acre park. They assisted with the $13,000 cost and constructed a lighted softball diamond.[49]

Trail Drivers' Park is the only park in Texas to honor the thousands of nameless cowboys who made history. Standing on a hillside overlooking the Trinity River, the park encompasses a site where these same brave fellows kept watch for Indians, prairie fires, or just rested after their herds crossed the muddy Trinity.[50]

3
Creating
Communities

Several communities make up Fort Worth's present North Side, but its roots really go back to the small community just north of the bluff that, in the 1890s, was called Marine.

Marine grew slowly, but once Armour and Swift arrived in 1902, the meat packing interests urged livestock people to incorporate a separate city surrounding the yards. Armour and Swift had already accomplished this task in other places around the country where they had established stockyards and packing plants — South St. Paul, Minnesota; South San Francisco, California; St. Joseph, Missouri, and others. The city of North Fort Worth officially became a separate entity in November, 1902, its boundaries stretching from Marine Creek on the north to the Trinity River on the south, and from the Santa Fe tracks on the east to Grand Avenue on the west.[1] The new city of 300 residents swallowed the little community of Marine. North Main and Twenty-fifth streets became the major commercial thoroughfares serving the area, but Central also remained important. The empty streets of the subdivision proposed by Nathan Barrett in 1888 rapidly filled with houses after 1902, and a thriving commercial district blossomed on North Main Street.[2]

Officials of the new city were mostly people with livestock interests. J. D. Farmer, a partner in a commission firm whose livestock livelihood would continue into three generations, served as the first mayor.[3]

By the spring of 1903, the city council had adopted a resolution prohibiting the hitching of horses on Main Street for longer than thirty minutes and reminded farmers bringing their livestock to market to take note. Perhaps the city fathers did not want the men to linger too long at Frenchy's Blue Goose Saloon.[4]

The council also adopted a resolution to expel "squatters" living in tents. People apparently were moving in faster than carpenters could construct houses. Furthermore, many of the immigrants from eastern Europe were "tenting up" to save money for down payments on their own homes rather than staying in the available boarding houses or renting from the "company." To expedite permanent settlement, the council announced that tent dwellers would be fined $10 for every day they stayed after being given notice to move.[5] North Fort Worth had begun taking itself seriously.

The growing community soon acquired its own city hall and jail, both contained in a single red brick building at the southeast corner of Twentieth Street and North Main. At the council meeting February 11, 1903, the members even presented Mayor Farmer with a beautiful wooden gavel with silver bands and a silver tip.[6] The council also authorized the construction of the two-story red brick M. G. Ellis school at Fourteenth and North Main in 1905.

North Fort Worth existed as an independent municipality for only a little over seven years — 1902-1909 — before being incorporated into the larger city of Fort Worth. During that brief period, however, it faced the same problems and concerns as any burgeoning frontier community, including law enforcement, budgets, and public policy.

Just before Christmas in 1903, the council passed an ordinance "prohibiting the shooting of firecrackers and Roman candles on Main and Rusk Streets, Central, Ellis, and Lake Avenue." Violators were subject to fine. This represented a considerable improvement over earlier days when citizens more frequently shot off six-shooters than Roman candles on Main Street.[7]

The following May, the council instructed the city attorney to draft an ordinance forbidding the use of slingshots in North Fort Worth and also "prohibiting leaving horses unhitched on streets and alleys and prohibiting same to awning posts or lamp posts or

First mayor of North Fort Worth and commission
man at the stockyards, J. D. Farmer (Fort Worth
Public Library).

fences."8 Some stockyards cowboys must have angered citizens; a
civilized city could not allow horses just anywhere. The next
month, the council passed an ordinance to prevent persons from
hopping steam cars while in motion.

The stockyards and related activities remained the city's major
industry and took precedence over all other considerations,
including the budget. At the March 13, 1906 meeting, the council authorized the city marshal to pay four extra policemen during
the livestock show. A couple of months later, the council accepted a bid to put a bridge across Marine Creek on Main Street for
$1,050. That fall, they extended Exchange Avenue west from

Main Street to Ellis Avenue and declared it a public street. Before that, Exchange Avenue was only a wide trail leading to the stockyards. The city upgraded its streets with sewers, gutters, sidewalks, and even lighting. A couple of years later the council even passed an ordinance against the cherished western habit of spitting on the sidewalks. Clearly, the twentieth century had arrived.[9]

An energetic young Jewish immigrant named Sam Rosen made a lasting impact on the community. In 1883, when he worked his way by ship from Kovarsk, Russia, to the U.S., young Rosen was twelve years old and could not even speak English. But he knew he was fleeing an oppressive government to seek a better life in America. His descendants agree that the last name Rosen was probably a shortened form of a longer Jewish name such as Rosenberg or Rosenbaum.

Young as he was and small in the bargain, Sam knew what he had to do: work hard and save his money. During his first year in America, Rosen joined his brother and worked for a farmer near Oak Cliff at Dallas seven days a week from dawn to dark for $5 per week. Although he saved nearly all of his wages, Rosen realized that hoeing corn and cotton and feeding the farm animals offered no job advancement. His boss, the farmer, worked as hard as he did. If he worked twenty years, he would still be doing the same thing, even if he bought his own farm.[10]

Rosen quit his job and got another as a clerk in a crockery store in Dallas, then later appeared in Fort Worth peddling novelties and jewelry. He often traveled westward from Fort Worth, sometimes reaching El Paso. In a few years he had saved enough to open a tiny dry goods store in a frame building on Fort Worth's Main Street. He chose a storefront between Eleventh and Twelfth streets down near the railroad station because of cheaper rental property there. The store was located in the section of town called "Hell's Half Acre," an area with an unsavory reputation as a vice and red-light district. Still, one had to start somewhere. After a few years, Rosen moved to a better location between Fifth and Sixth streets and continued the mercantile business there for the next eleven years.[11]

As the twentieth century arrived, Rosen began seeing developments north of the Trinity River. Having continued to save his

Sam Rosen (at right), the developer of Rosen Heights, with his
wife and son Ephraim. Son Joel was away at college when this
photograph was taken in the 1920s (courtesy Sam and Ron
Rosen, grandsons).

money, Rosen was ready when rumors spread in 1901 that Armour and Swift planned to build modern plants. Prowling North Main Street, he looked around for land to purchase as an investment. Fortunately, he made his move before the packer-owned North Fort Worth Townsite Company, represented by Joe Googins, began buying up everything in sight. Thirty-year-old Sam Rosen purchased a 320-acre farm just west of North Main Street, at present Twenty-fifth Street. His property was bordered on the north and west with the Sansom Ranch, on the east with the stockyards, and on the south with the Marine Addition.[12] He planned to divide it into lot-sized tracts for resale and to call the area Rosen Heights. In 1903, he sold his store in downtown Fort Worth to devote full-time to his real estate business.[13]

Although Rosen chose to be a developer, not a builder, he constructed a few houses as rental property. Mainly, however, he sold plots of land. His ads proclaimed: "Buy a Lot in God's Country. Rosen Heights is Level, High, Dry, Healthy and Invigorating."[14]

He priced his lots from $250 to $400, and one could purchase a lot for $15 down and $5 per month. He even "sacrificed" eighty lots at $100 each.[15]

Because few people possessed cars in 1902, Rosen included a promise with each lot sold that there soon would be streetcar service from Rosen Heights into downtown Fort Worth. Many newcomers took advantage of his sales and promises, and within a year, 150 families enjoyed new houses built on lots in Rosen Heights. Rosen moved about his new development, visiting and tipping his little black hat to residents.

In March 1904, Rosen appeared before the North Fort Worth City Council requesting a franchise to provide electric light service to North Fort Worth. The following month the city granted his request on the condition that the city receive its own electricity at cost.[16] Then in October of that same year, on behalf of the North Fort Worth and Rosen Heights Street Railway Company, Rosen appeared again before the city council, this time seeking a franchise to lay streetcar track on certain city streets. The city approved that request as well.

In Rosen's plans for his streetcar line, he intended to work out an arrangement with the Northern Texas Traction Company which already operated a line up North Main Street to the stock-yards. Northern's owners had used several existing electric car lines to create the company in about 1900; it had twenty-two miles of electric lines operating in Fort Worth by 1901. Rosen wanted to build a line to connect his housing addition to the existing line; then his Rosen Heights residents could ride all the way from their front door to the downtown area with only one transfer to the Northern Traction line.

Optimistically, Rosen broke ground for his own line, beginning at the 2800 block of Azle Avenue in the western portion of his addition. But, when he tried to make arrangements with the Northern Texas Traction Company to connect the two lines, company officials refused to cooperate. Devastated, Rosen saw his plans about to fail. Many people had purchased land with his promise of streetcar service to downtown as the deciding factor. Rosen, of course, saw the necessity for the streetcar line as not only the fulfillment of a promise but as the key to continued development.

His residents would have to pay two fares to reach downtown if he could not make some other arrangement. He even offered to pay the five cent fares for his own people to transfer to the Northern cars; thus Northern would actually have gained business from Rosen's residents. Yet, since the owners of Northern rejected this offer, Rosen saw no other option but to build his own street-car line all the way into Fort Worth.

He obtained franchises from both cities to build. Rosen began first to lay track north-south in downtown Fort Worth, east of Main Street, running the entire length of downtown. As he built northward, he faced more formidable construction problems. The construction of a steel bridge over the Trinity presented a major task. This eventually accomplished, his track entered the North Side and then he faced another challenge. His track paralleled Northern's on North Main Street as far as the stockyards, but then would have to cross the Northern line west of his own to reach the western part of his addition. Northern adamantly refused to grant permission for Rosen to turn west and cross their track. Somehow Rosen had to find a way to cross the opposition's line.

A legend has grown up about how Rosen finally accomplished

this feat. Apparently he kept his men working around the clock one wintry night in 1905 in the middle of a snowstorm so severe that Northern's officials did not suspect anyone of being out, much less working on the track. The only way that Rosen's construction foremen could keep their men on the job throughout the freezing night was by intermittently serving them whiskey and coffee. Lowenstein's Saloon at the corner of Exchange Avenue and North Main remained open all night to help. Whenever the work started slowing down and the men began complaining too loudly of the cold and wet, the foreman would make a run to the saloon for more coffee and "antifreeze" to fortify the crews.

The next morning when North Siders went to work, they found the Fort Worth and Rosen Heights Street Railway Company track crossing that of the Northern Texas Traction Company and connected with the line extending westward into Rosen Heights. Rosen had finally completed the entire line and opened for business. He and his men had exhibited the same sort of "can-do" spirit that had earlier brought the stockyards and the packing plants to North Fort Worth.

As one might expect, the Northern Texas Traction Company did not take too kindly to its right of way being compromised, nor to losing profits to an upstart company. Competition continued between the two streetcar lines, for both carried passengers all the way into Fort Worth, the Northern Texas Company crossing the Trinity on a wooden bridge west of the present North Main Street viaduct. Cars often raced when they found themselves on the parallel part of the line on North Main Street between the Trinity River and the stockyards. Of course, both managements officially frowned on such shenanigans.

When a big show played at the Opera House on Third Street downtown, streetcars tried to accommodate their North Side patrons. If as many as ten patrons attended from the North Side and notified the company, the car would wait. If they forgot to notify the company, they had to walk home.[17] Both streetcar lines could afford to be magnanimous; they enjoyed their busiest periods morning and evening carrying workers to the Armour and Swift plants.

When his dreams did not match his means, Sam Rosen repeatedly proved to be a man of ingenuity. Seeing the opportunity to expand into a Rosen Heights Phase II by purchasing additional land, he enlisted the financial support of his in-laws in Beaumont, Texas. Rosen had married Betty Gordon in 1896. He found his father-in-law and a brother-in-law willing to become involved. With their help, he purchased a 1,171 acre tract just northwest of his original addition.[18] Some of the streets in the new addition are named after these in-laws and Rosen's own two sons. These include Ephriham (although he spelled his son's name Ephraim), Pearl (after his brother-in-law Perlstein), Hannah, and a Gordon Street to honor his father-in-law and his wife's maiden name.

Gordon Street was a major thoroughfare for a time, but because a Gordon Street already existed in south Fort Worth, the city of Fort Worth changed it when Rosen Heights later became a part of the larger city. "Mother got upset over the name change," explained Joel, one of Rosen's sons. "She circulated a petition asking the city to change the name of the South Side Gordon Street and leave the North Side Gordon as it was."[19] Betty Gordon Rosen lost out, however, for the city renamed the street "Long Avenue" because it was one of the longest streets in the area.

Rosen donated land at Northwest Twenty-sixth Street and Roosevelt for a school called Sam Rosen Elementary. Rosen even built an amusement park to benefit the residents of his additions and to encourage more use of the streetcar line by Fort Worthians. Officially named Rosen Heights Amusement Park, it included a fifty-acre artificial lake. People began calling the area White City because of the white buildings and the bright lights that shone out from it at night, illuminating the entire area.

Rosen also built four large water tanks to supply his residents. He offered people all the water they wanted if they would plant trees and flowers. Many took him up on the offer, and as a result a brightly colored oasis soon bloomed northwest of North Main Street.

Presumably, some of the new homes in Rosen Heights put in permanent bathtubs. Sam Smith, whose family moved to Marine in 1895 when Sam was twelve, remembered that the very first bathtubs stood in barber shops. One could go to a barber shop on Saturday, carry a change of clothes, and take a bath for a quarter with the soap and towel included.[20]

A *Fort Worth Telegram* account of the new Rosen Heights development bragged: "On the Heights are to be found the better class of people. Here one can find doctors, lawyers, government men employed in the packing plants, merchants of Fort Worth who would rather live at Rosen Heights than down in the city, and men of all professions and trades."[21] The citizens of the area covered the complete socioeconomic spectrum, however, and at one end were the employees of the packing houses. In fact, the opening of the plants was Rosen's incentive for choosing the area in the first place and certainly contributed to its rapid growth. By 1906, in fact, when Rosen was still only in his late thirties, his development represented the most rapidly growing area of the city. By contrast, another turn-of-the-century suburban development west of Fort Worth, Arlington Heights, grew much more slowly and did not surpass Rosen Heights until much later, although the city was gradually growing in a westerly direction. Arlington Heights had fewer businesses that could provide jobs than Rosen Heights and the area north of the Trinity. In the days before the prevalence of automobiles, folks preferred living near their employment.

Many of Rosen's residents bought homes on the installment plan, but some dipped into savings and purchased outright. The area seemed especially attractive because of the liberal zoning laws. People were at liberty to raise chickens and have pets on their property. Many also kept cows, giving the neighborhood a rural flavor.

Young families bought lots from Sam Rosen, contracted for the construction of houses, and moved in. As they tended their chickens, orchards, and gardens at the back of their houses, they became acquainted with their neighbors. They bought "Light Crust Flour" from North Side's Burrus Mill and Elevator Company. Some even put in telephone service, paying $1 per month.[22] They could take their laundry to the North Side Penny Laundry, located on the corner of Exchange Avenue and North Main Street. Men could get their collars and cuffs washed and starched for one and one-half cents each and a shirt washed and starched for eight cents.[23] Residents with a little extra cash and a yen for music saw the Edison phonograph advertisements in the

*Relaxing at White City in Rosen Heights, which was available by
streetcar, became the in thing to do. This photo was made about
1907 (courtesy of Robert and Barty Duncan).*

newspaper and purchased one to the delight or dismay of neighbors who heard its strains blare forth through open windows on
summer evenings.

Rosen's Beaumont in-laws began building houses to sell on
some of the lots. Prices ranged from $750 to $1,000. Better houses
sold for $1,000 to $5,000. Rosen advertised lots for $2.50 per
month with no interest or taxes.[24]

People came to the Rosen Heights Land Company office, first
located on North Main Street and later at 312 Northwest Twenty-
fifth Street, to make their water bill payments and to pay on their
mortgage notes. Rosen's grandsons claim that Sam never fore-
closed on a single mortgage during all the years of his real estate
operation. When someone complained to Rosen about a land purchase, he offered to give their money back. Rosen, and later his

sons Joel and Ephraim, allowed people to live in houses for free rather than permit the houses to stand vacant during the Depression. Residents just paid what they could.[25]

Those who came to the Rosen office to pay on their notes met a lady named Margaret Dewer whom everyone called "Miss Maggie." For sixty-seven years, from 1906 to 1973, she worked six days a week for the Rosens, taking only one vacation during all those years. In the early days, she traveled by train to Laguna Beach, California. Apparently, after having seen California, she thought her life complete; she had "seen the elephant," as they used to say in the Old West. She never again asked for time off from her duties and worked until ten days before her death at age eighty-eight.[26]

In 1906, the Northern Texas Traction Company bought out Sam Rosen's streetcar line and another competitor. Two years later, the company was grossing $1.25 million a year, with fares at only five cents apiece.[27] Most of these profits came from North Side residents.

With the stockyards booming and Rosen Heights expanding, more and more families arrived in the growing community of North Fort Worth. One of these was the Robert Lee Bradford family who moved from the Riverside area where he had been a truck farmer. Bradford bought land in far northwest Rosen Heights on Azle Avenue and got a job with Northern Texas Traction Company. Bradford would drive the streetcar to the end of the line and leave it, walking the mile or so home. The next morning he would walk to the streetcar and pick up other men who worked for the same company as he drove in toward town on his first run. Often he performed the job of "tripper," which meant he would stand on the curb making change so people would have the correct amount to pay when they got on the streetcar. This was important early in the morning when several streetcars lined up as hundreds of North Side workers hurried to their jobs.[28]

To the west of the Bradford house stretched open fields and the Marion Sansom Ranch. Like most ranchers, Sansom would drive cattle in to the stockyards from his ranch. Each Saturday, Bradford's wife, son, and daughter Louise walked the mile from their house to the streetcar line. One Saturday they had only

*This Longhorn at the Fort Worth stockyards had horns stretching
seven feet one inch from tip to tip. Occasionally steers escaped
from the yards and chased people (courtesy Robert and Barty
Duncan).*

walked a block when they saw a white-faced red bull that had
become separated from a herd. Five-year-old Louise was wearing a
red coat with brass buttons. Believing that the red might anger
the bull, Mrs. Bradford jerked Louise's coat off and tucked it under
her own long skirt. She lifted Louise over a nearby fence, hoisted
Louise's three-year-old brother, and then climbed over herself,
barely making it before the bull charged the fence, pawing the
earth and bawling. They stayed on the other side of the fence
until a neighbor rescued them. They did not get to make their
usual trip to downtown Fort Worth that day.[29]

When Louise was in the fifth grade, the family moved closer in
to Rosen Avenue and lived three doors down from Sam Rosen
and his family. She knew Ephraim and Joel and remembered
roller-skating on the sidewalk in front of the Rosen house and Joel

coming out and giving her a kosher dill pickle that his mother had canned.[30]

Family after family continued to arrive and by the end of the first decade of the twentieth century, a thriving community existed in the little city of North Fort Worth. The city that the packers had urged residents to incorporate grew rapidly as the stockyards and packing plants kept expanding facilities and hiring more workers.

By 1909, the city of Fort Worth became anxious to incorporate the growing North Fort Worth area, including Rosen Heights, into the city limits. During this time, the state legislature could merge incorporated cities whenever it chose. Fort Worth Mayor W. D. Harris and the city commissioners urged State Representative Louis J. Wortham of Fort Worth to request such an incorporation. Wortham introduced a private bill to do so. This high-handed action came as a complete surprise to the city of North Fort Worth. During their last city council meeting on March 9, 1909, the aldermen gave no indication that they knew that annexation was imminent, for they ratified purchase of two lots for new fire halls. This was not the action of a city of 16,000 planing on going out of business very soon. But Fort Worth prevailed and annexed North Fort Worth, although city officials purposely left the industrial area of the stockyards and packing plants outside the city limits, and thus outside the taxing area, with a plan to attract even more businesses to the North Side.[31]

The city officials hoped that other packing plants and businesses would move to the tax-free area. The Fort Worth Chamber of Commerce advertised in many trade journals throughout the United States, but the response did not meet expectations. Consequently, in 1911, officials prepared to annex the small but wealthy industrial area in order to place it within Fort Worth's tax base.

Thirty-three men assembled hurriedly in T. E. "Dad" Carson's grocery store at 126 Decatur Avenue after worried livestock interests and local businessmen resolved to forestall Fort Worth's threatened annexation. The men had a major undertaking in mind: to incorporate the one-half mile area which included the stockyards, the packing plants, and a few houses and stores into a separate city. With the knowledge that the absentee stockyards and meat-packing owners supported them, the men voted 33-0 in favor of incorporation.

The next topic of discussion concerned naming their tiny municipality. Someone suggested "Carson City" after the elderly Carson, but that name would have conflicted with a similar town in Nevada. Carson suggested that they name their city after the man most of them credited with bringing Armour and Swift to Fort Worth: Louville V. Niles.

Niles' negotiations and those of his partner, Greenlief W. Simpson, had brought the meat-packers to town. Because Niles had spent time in Fort Worth trying to make a success of the packing plant, he was given more credit than Simpson, who had remained in Boston. The men reasoned Niles's vision, business sense, and aggressive salesmanship had created their prosperous little community.[32] Although Niles had no part in naming the city which honored him, he was appreciative and visited every year during the fat stock show until 1928, the last year of his life.[33]

The incorporated community of Niles City boasted, besides the stockyards and packing plants, a police and fire department, artesian wells, electricity, telephone and gas service, five schools, two grain elevators, a pottery works, a roundhouse for the railroad, three grocery stores, and one drugstore. This impressive inventory caused Fort Worth to cast covetous eyes on its neighbor in years to come. These same assets also allowed Niles City to maintain its independence and to prosper in the shadow of Fort Worth for several years before the larger city swallowed it up for tax reasons.[34]

The men who met to form Niles City saw only a bright future for their experiment in city-making. They chose Carson as the first mayor in the April 1911 elections.[35] The little community soon took on the title of "richest little city in the U.S." because the high property values of the livestock interests in comparison to the small population made the per capita worth around $50,000 for each man, woman, and child.

The following year city aldermen purchased a lot and constructed a brick and stucco city hall on Decatur Avenue at a cost of $4,511.[36] The Fort Worth Stock Yards Company began building rent houses for their employees and those of the packing plants.

*The Niles City municipal building (1911-1923) fell into disuse
and was torn down to make space for a parking lot in 1975
(North Fort Worth Historical Society).*

They constructed seventy of these within a decade and rented
them out at low prices.

Some citizens of North Fort Worth and Niles City remained
angry that the city of Fort Worth had annexed North Fort Worth.
They wanted a newspaper which would serve the needs of the
entire North Fort Worth area and help the community retain its
separate identity. Thus, later that same year, several prominent
men approached the stockyards management, who published the
livestock newspaper, asking their help. The result was the *North
Fort Worth News*, born in November 1911. M. L. McCain, Jr., who
had formerly served as city editor of the *Fort Worth Record*,
became the first editor of the *News*.[37]

Fort Worth still wanted Niles City within its own limits so that
the valuable stockyards and meat-packing properties would be
inside its tax base. Wallace Malone, the state representative from
Fort Worth, introduced in 1919 a thinly disguised bill to permit a

Above, young women learn to cook in a home economics class at Diamond Hill High School. The year is 1916 (North Fort Worth Historical Society).

city of a 100,000 to 150,000 population (Fort Worth) to annex an adjacent city with less than a 2,000 population (Niles City). The bill failed, mainly because some board members of the Diamond Hill Independent School District strongly protested. Malone reintroduced his bill the next year, but Niles City officials attempted to forestall the action by increasing their boundaries and thus their population to more than 2,000. The Niles City aldermen extended the city limits outward by .93 square miles, making the maximum incorporated limits of Niles City 1.5 square miles. The newly annexed area included Diamond Hill, North Fostepco Heights, and Washington Heights, and boosted the official population to 2,600, sufficient to escape Malone's bill.[38]

The city of Fort Worth ignored the aldermen's action and annexed the area anyway on July 22, 1922. Fort Worth claimed that Niles City added to their territory just to nullify the law.

Niles City challenged in court, lost the first round, and appealed to the circuit court.[39]

Unfortunately, the biggest taxpayers, the stockyards and the packers, quit paying any taxes to Niles City after the court fight began, preferring to adopt a wait-and-see attitude. This left the city administration unable to pay its bills. The appeals case was still pending in July 1923 when Fort Worth and Niles City reached an out-of-court settlement. Niles City would drop the protest if Fort Worth would assume the debts of the smaller city.[40]

With the annexation of Niles City into Fort Worth, all of the area that had originally been North Fort Worth, including the stockyards district, came into the boundaries of the larger city. More challenges would come to the North Side, but her citizens would face them as a part of the City of Fort Worth.

4
An Ethnic Pot Melts, Sort Of

In the seventy-five years from 1815 to 1890, only fifteen million people immigrated to the United States, mostly from western Europe. By 1890, however, sailing costs had decreased, and steamship companies began serving new ports in Italy or the Baltic, bringing passengers to America in ten days. Consequently, the next twenty-four years brought another fifteen million immigrants, this time mostly from southern and eastern Europe.[1]

Early immigrants homesteaded farmland in the Midwest; because little land remained after 1890, however, newer immigrants flocked to the cities for work. The average wage for workers in most small European countries at the turn of the century was only $25 to $30 per year. In the U.S., an able-bodied man with practically no skill in any type of work could earn twice that amount in a month.[2] Flight from religious or racial persecution, however, probably motivated more newcomers than the greater economic opportunity found in America.[3] Yet no matter why they came, they fulfilled J. Hector St. John de Crevecoeur's 1782 prophesy that "here individuals of all nations are melted into a new race of men, whose labors and posterity will one day cause great changes in the world."[4]

The North Side immigrants had dreamed of America from their crowded Old World cities and their overfarmed rural districts. Some had lived in several other U.S. cities before settling down in North Fort Worth; others came directly to the stockyards area by train after their boat docked in New York City or Galveston. Some left families in Europe and planned to work just long enough to earn money to send or take back home with them. Others brought their families along or sent for them as soon as they could earn the passage money.[5] As these immigrants found homes around the stockyards and packing plants, they contributed to the North Side's distinctive culture and its feelings of separateness from neighboring Fort Worth.

Fort Worth's melting pot was located between Calhoun and Commerce streets and Twenty-second and Twenty-third in the first decade of the twentieth century. The first generation immigrants spoke a dozen languages, married only within their own nationality, and retained a great deal of their Old World customs. Their children, however, spoke "mostly English and [had] girlfriends or boyfriends from any race."[6]

Anglo residents of the North Side referred to the newcomers as "Bohunks" regardless of which central or eastern European country they had called home. Bohemia was indeed the motherland of many of the immigrants, but others came from Slovakia, Austria, Serbia, Romania, Italy, Poland, Greece, Croatia, Russia, and half a dozen other homelands.[7]

A Russian immigrant named Meyer Greines arrived in North Fort Worth in 1905 and started a small furniture store in the southwest corner of the two-story Rosen Inn, located on the 1300 block of North Main Street. Eventually his store expanded until it included the entire building.

Greines was born in Minsk, Russia, in 1857; his wife Sarah, also Russian, was born six years later. They met and married in the "old country," and several of their children were born there. The family decided to come to America in the early 1890s, entering at Ellis Island. Sarah gave birth to another child in New York City. Meyer and Sarah did not want to remain in the crowded East, however, so they settled in New Mexico Territory for a time, then Corsicana, Texas, and next, Tyler. New babies arrived periodically.

In Tyler, Greines entered the furniture business quite by accident. He had been following a profession familiar to many Jewish immigrants: peddling. Many immigrants found a stepping stone to a more profitable profession by traveling and selling a small stock of merchandise. While the Greines family lived in Tyler, someone traded Greines a bed that he really did not need; he later considered this to be his entry into the business that he would follow the rest of his life.

When Greines moved his family to North Fort Worth, he rented a small house on Lee Street which proved too tiny for their family of eight. David, one of a set of twin boys, explored the neighborhood and found a larger house for sale at 1317 Circle Park Boulevard. Greines purchased the house for his family, and he and his wife and sons lived in it the remainder of their lives. Only Greines's sole daughter, Ida, married and moved elsewhere. Before she married, Ida taught school at Denver Avenue Elementary. In those days the schools conducted Bible reading each morning to start the day. Frequently, the scripture would be about Jesus from the New Testament. When this happened, Ida would step out of the room and let another teacher take over until the devotional concluded.[8]

Greines Furniture Store on North Main Street provided a livelihood for Meyer and Sarah, their oldest son Mose, and their daughter Ida and her husband, Adolph Cohen. Meyer also made some profitable real estate investments along the way. The family lived quite comfortably, and most of the boys attended college and went on to respected professions. During the last years of his life, Greines sat at the front of the store and greeted customers as they came into the building. He turned most of the operation of the business over to Mose, but enjoyed visiting with friends and customers he had met during the years. The white-haired man with the long, snowy beard became a familiar fixture at the front of the store. "Come in, son," he greeted each man. He called everyone "son" whether they truly were young or near his own age. Greines died in 1937, and his wife Sarah followed ten years later.[9]

Many persons wondered why the five Greines boys — Mose, Jake, Abe, David, and Sol — never married. One theory speculated that their mother always urged them not to marry until they could find a "nice Jewish girl," and Jewish families remained scarce in North Fort Worth at that time. Also, Meyer and Sarah never enjoyed good health, and the boys felt a responsibility to take care of them. The twins, David and Sol, became lawyers with

Greines Furniture Store started in a corner of a building in the 1300 block (above) of North Main. The business later expanded to fill the entire structure (courtesy Robert and Barty Duncan).

offices downtown, but they stopped by the store every day on their way home and handled the legal aspects of the family business. Abe practiced medicine in the North Fort Worth community for sixty years, and Jake ran a dry-goods store up the street from his parents' business.

The Greines family was always eager to help their adopted community. Greines Furniture Store did not charge interest when customers took their time paying for furniture. Mose Greines always said, "Just pay when you can."[10] Abe, Sol, and David frequently donated their professional services to poor families. According to a popular story on the North Side, whenever a poor client would ask Sol how much was owed, Sol would shrug and say, "Just bring me some chicken and dumplings."[11] Abe also donated the land which became Greines Field in the 1500 block of North Main Street. When young men and women needed clothes to graduate from high school, Jake would call them in and let them have what they needed. He assured them that they could repay him after they graduated and got a job. "The Greines were like second parents to the young people growing up in North Fort

Worth," one such youngster, Esmond Scarborough, remembered later.[12]

Influences from the old country flavored social and religious activities among the many immigrant residents. One early meeting place on the near North Side was a *biergarten* near the site of the present electric power generators where the Clear and the West forks of the Trinity River meet. Promoters of the *biergarten* constructed an open-air pavilion in 1900 in the 300 block of North Main Street among some large trees and called their gathering place Hermann Park.[13] The German Society, called the *Deutscher Verein*, or Sons of Hermann, sponsored activities at the park which provided a rendezvous for the German population of the entire city of Fort Worth. Folks enjoyed gathering on Saturday or Sunday evenings during the first decade of the twentieth century, the heyday of the park.[14]

As the weather grew warmer in the spring and events could be held in the open-air pavilion, the *Deutscher Verein* would send their German band in a parade through the residential sections of Fort Worth. They would promenade from block to block playing "Blue Danube" and other Strauss waltzes and Viennese music. Citizens heard the music wafting in through their open windows, knowing that they were getting only a teaser of the many strains and melodies they could enjoy if they traveled out to the pavilion for the opening kick-off of the new season: a three-day May festival and the crowning of a queen.[15] As the band tramped up and down the streets, it always attracted a considerable following of small boys. Often each little boy had a dog, and the parade got longer and livelier as it continued along.[16]

When the band led the crowd back to Hermann Park, many North Siders waited under the pavilion for the festivities. The park was a place for young people to go on a date or meet others their age. Many loved to dance to the lively waltzes and polkas. Some of the older folks just liked to visit with their friends and watch the young dancers.

One couple who met at Hermann Park Beer Garden and Dance

Pavilion was Joseph Milankovich and Anna Obal, both immigrants from central Europe. Joseph came to the United States
when he was only fifteen from the part of the old Austria-
Hungarian Empire that later would be Yugoslavia. He first traveled to St. Louis because he had a sister living there. In St. Louis
he played in the band of a traveling Wild West show.
Unfortunately, the show went bankrupt in Temple, Texas, and dis-
missed everyone. The manager told the band members that he
had heard that jobs existed at the packing plants in Fort Worth
and suggested that they go there and work at least long enough to
earn their fare back to St. Louis. Most of the young men did
exactly that, but Joseph chose to remain in Fort Worth. Perhaps
Anna was the reason. She and her father had come from the
Moravian region of Czechoslovakia in 1910 to join several cousins
and friends already living in North Fort Worth.

After meeting at the park and becoming well acquainted,
Joseph and Anna wanted to marry, but they did not have enough
money. One evening when they got off the streetcar on the way to
Hermann Park, a taxi hit them. Fortunately, they were not hurt,
but the cab company gave them $100 anyway. This windfall
allowed them to proceed with their marriage plans.

Joseph Milankovich loved music and continued to play with
various bands in Fort Worth, including the Shrine Band. Several
years later, after his children entered the North Side schools,
Milankovich decided to shorten — to "Americanize" — his name.
Thus it became Milan, making it easier for his children to adjust
in school. Many other immigrants did the same.[17]

A friend of Joseph and Anna named Joseph Becan had been
born in the Ukraine to Czech parents. Becan's family came to Fort
Worth in 1905 when he was only thirteen. The next year he
began working in one of the meat packing plants for twelve cents
an hour, ten hours a day, six days a week. Some of the native
Texans disparagingly called him a "Bohunk," as they did many of
the central and eastern European immigrants. This kind of dis-
criminatory treatment caused the Slavic immigrants to become

clannish and to support each other more so than they would have done otherwise.

One result of the support-system formed in North Fort Worth's Czech community was the Sokol organization. Dr. Miroslav Tyrs, a professor of art history at Charles University in Prague, founded Sokol in 1862 to give his enslaved nation (which had been under Austrian rule since 1620) a means to work toward freedom "through a physical, moral, and spiritual regeneration."[18] The organization was brought to the U.S. by Czech immigrants three years later. Joseph Milan and Joseph Becan helped form a local chapter in North Fort Worth which began teaching — through gymnastics — patriotism, clean and healthy living, and self-discipline to young people of the Czech community.

In Czechoslovakia, Adolph Hitler dissolved the patriotic organization after he took control in 1938. Czechs resumed Sokol after World War II, but when the communists gained control in 1948, Sokol was outlawed again. For four decades Sokol existed only in the Free World in such places as the North Side of Fort Worth where it remains active today.

Milan and Joseph Becan founded the first Fort Worth Sokol in 1913 after a group meeting of several friends in Becan's back yard. They joined with a Czech fraternal insurance organization, the Slavonic Benevolent Order of the State of Texas, and constructed a lodge at 2400 North Houston Street. The Czech-language insurance organization, founded in 1896 at LaGrange, Texas, provided reliable and inexpensive death benefits to immigrants so that they did not have to risk being at the mercy of unethical insurance salesmen who often took advantage of non-English speaking newcomers. In 1974, the Sokol organization and insurance Lodge No. 154 constructed the large Eagle Mountain Athletic Club at 6500 Boat Club Road for family gatherings and gymnastic competitions (called *slets*) for the youngsters. The St. Thomas the Apostle Catholic Church, dedicated in its present location at 2920 Azle Avenue on December 5, 1937, was a Czech-language church until the 1950s.[19]

The history of one Czech family is particularly interesting. The Karel Haba family arrived in Fort Worth in 1916, and Karel operated a saloon on North Twenty-fifth Street. After Prohibition forced him out of business, the family returned to Czechoslovakia, except for two older children who had married here. When Karel Haba died in a farm accident, his widow returned to the United States with the two youngest children, this time leaving two older ones in Czechoslovakia. This separation of the family by an ocean and two continents kept loyalties and emotions divided for many years. [20]

Along with business-oriented Russian Jews and patriotic Sokol-loving Czechs, Greek immigrants also migrated to the North Side. The first to arrive was Demetrios Anagnostakis, who came from Crete in 1893, with a wish to be a cowboy. The nearest he came to punching cows was working as a yard man in the cattle pens of commission agents at the Fort Worth Stockyards. By 1911, about 200 other young men — mostly single — fled Greece and came to Fort Worth to escape Turkish oppression. Most secured jobs in the packing plants initially. The early Greek immigrants were poor and had limited education and skills because they came primarily from agricultural communities. They left their families in Greece because they did not plan to stay in America. Their intention was to earn some money and go home.[21] Yet, because they often met and married young Fort Worth ladies — and for other reasons — many stayed.

By the 1930s, about seventy-five percent of the Greeks in Fort Worth had become truck farmers. They saved their packing-house wages and purchased land, taking the lead in the development of truck farming in the Trinity River bottoms. The other twenty-five percent of the Greeks owned small businesses.[22]

One of the young Greeks who came to the U.S. in this early migration was Fideris Sparto. He began calling himself "Jim" soon after he arrived in Fort Worth in 1912. Sparto's brother, who was already here, helped him get a job at Swift. Jim worked hard and saved his money. He met a young lady named Muscola Vloitos who came to live with her two brothers in 1916. The two soon married and rented land near White Settlement Road. Later, Sparto bought property northeast of the West Fork Bridge and south of Oakwood Cemetery. He and his family worked the land until the 1980s, growing beets, carrots, onions, mustard greens, okra, and similar truck-garden crops. They sold their produce at a

The Haba family before they came to America: left to right, Mary, Anna, Mrs. Karel (Anna), Karel and Louis; the youngest child in front is Jerry (courtesy Millie Crow, daughter of Millie Haba Wruble).

farmers' market on Jones Street in downtown Fort Worth for many years. Later they contracted with grocery stores and delivered fresh vegetables. Mary Sparto, a daughter of Jim and Muscola, noted that the first generation of Greeks who came to Fort Worth worked the truck farms and their children did too. "But the third generation went to college and got other jobs," she said.[23]

Another family of long-time Greek truck farmers were the Pappajohns. George, born in 1880 in Greece, came to the U.S. in about 1912, working first for the packing house and even for a railroad for a short while. He brought a young family with him; his son Steve was five. Soon George rented land all up and down the Trinity River on which to farm. By 1934, the Pappajohns had purchased their own land along the Trinity near Rockwood Golf Course, just south of the Jacksboro Highway on Ohio Garden Road. The families did not go hungry during the Depression because of all the vegetables they raised for sale.[24] The third generation, Steve's sons, still truck farm in the 1990s, selling vegetables at their own produce market on Ohio Garden Road and also selling to wholesalers.

George Salicos came to the North Side in 1912 from a little community located about fifty miles from Smyrna on the Mediterranean, an area noted for its agriculture. He followed the pattern of his fellow Greeks and worked in one of the packing plants first, next delivered milk with a partner, and then rented farm land until the 1930s. By that time, Salicos could finally afford to purchase about eight acres on the Trinity River near Samuels Avenue. Salicos lived on his land, had a well, and irrigated out of the Trinity River. With all the vegetables that were in season nine or ten months a year, the family had plenty to sell and eat during the lean Depression years.[25]

Some of the Greek immigrants on the North Side met with other of their Fort Worth countrymen in January 1911 to establish the first Greek Orthodox Church in Fort Worth. At first they rented space on the second floor of a downtown building at

Weatherford and Houston streets, even though most of the members of the new church lived north of the river. They named their church the St. Demetrios Greek Orthodox Church after the first Greek to arrive in Fort Worth nearly two decades earlier.

Young Greeks who worked downtown purchased land at Tenth and Cherry streets in the southwest part of the downtown area for a church. This did not suit the majority of the Greek immigrants who lived on the North Side. They expressed their dissatisfaction so thoroughly and continually that finally the Greek businessmen sold the original property and paid $750 for another lot at 2022 Ross Avenue, north of the river. In 1917, members of the church laid the cornerstone. Their first permanent priest was Damianos Ermogenis. Within a few years, the church established after-school Greek language classes for the children of the parish.[26]

Mrs. Artemis Smith, one of the parishioners in the 1960s, proposed an idea that grew and developed into a tradition that still delights more people than just the members of the North Side Greek community. She suggested a fairly modest bread and pastry sale to acquaint the community with Greek baking and to help raise funds for the church. The bake sale has grown into the annual Greek Festival that the church still hosts at its modern community center at the corner of Twenty-first Street and Jacksboro Highway.

As the twentieth century progressed into its second decade, new businesses began to appear in North Fort Worth. European immigrants took every opportunity to grasp the American dream, utilize the free enterprise system, and make their life better in America than it had been in the old country. Like Sam Rosen and others before them, they became hard-working entrepreneurs.

On the very day that Harry and Sarah Jacobson arrived in town — March 19, 1919 — they bought out a dry-goods business from Jack Engler. Jacobson, born in Romania in 1888, came to the United States in 1906, settling in Chicago because an older brother lived there. He kept up with his family back home but never had enough time or money to go back for a visit. In

Chicago, he worked as a dishwasher in a restaurant. Riding the streetcar cost five cents, but he chose to walk the several miles to and from work in order to save that nickel twice a day. Harry and his brother soon moved to Dallas, where Harry obtained work in the Adolphus Hotel coffee shop.

He met Sarah Bress — who, with her family, had migrated from Russia as a small child — and the two married in 1913. The Jacobsons then moved to Britton, Texas (near Midlothian), for a time. There their children, sons Hyman and Meyer, were born. When they began their store on the North Side, they carried a little bit of everything in men's, women's, and children's clothing and shoes. The Jacobson dry-goods store was located for thirty-two years at 2385 North Main Street on the west side of the road. Because they needed more room, the business moved to 2400 North Main in 1951.

Harry and Sarah worked at the store side by side until Harry passed away in 1959. Sarah came to the store each day a little while longer and then stayed home to enjoy her children and grandchildren until she died in 1982. Her oldest son Hyman and his family took over operation of the store and changed the merchandise to men's western-style clothing in 1977, to take advantage of the continual stream of tourists to the stockyards area.[27]

Other immigrants besides the Jacobsons also saved their money and started small businesses near the stockyards. By 1920, a young fellow named Theo Yardanoff managed to purchase a small cafe on Northeast Twenty-third Street. His story is one of ingenuity and hard work, like that of many other North Side pioneers. Orphaned at a young age in his native Macedonia, a region in the present Yugoslavia, he worked and saved to come to America. After paying for his boat ticket across the Atlantic and his train ticket to Fort Worth, he arrived on the North Side with $400. He chose Fort Worth because he had an uncle living there.

Yardanoff found a place to live in the stockyards area where about 500 other Yugoslavs had come to work in the meat packing plants. He did not work there, however, but got a job as a janitor at Harris Hospital. He worked ten hours a day, six days a week, for fifty cents a day. Even so, he saved money.

Yardanoff wanted to take advantage of the opportunities America offered by going into business for himself, following the same path to success that Sam Rosen, Meyer Greines, and Harry Jacobson had trod before him. He took the first step by studying English at night after he got off work.

When Yardanoff opened his small cafe in 1920, he preferred to go over to the packing plants personally to pick out meats. Europeans traditionally ate more organ meats than Americans — liver, calf brains, and sweetbreads — so he did not rule anything out. One day, however, a cowboy came in and ordered "calf fries."

"What do you mean, 'calf fries'?" Yardanoff is said to have asked.

"They are what separates the bulls from the cows," the cowboy explained indulgently.[28]

With this knowledge, Yardanoff went to the packing house manager and asked how much they would charge per pound for the male parts.

"You can have them for nothing if you will carry them away," he was told.[29] So Yardanoff began carrying them away. He devised a calf-fry sandwich which he sold for fifteen cents. The cowboys and other adventurous customers loved it. Theo Yardanoff had created a culinary legend though it was ironic that it took a Yugoslav immigrant to popularize a "traditional" western dish.

Yardanoff eventually met a Polish immigrant named Josephine, and they were married. They had three children, Theo, Jr., Helen, and Wanda. In 1942, Theo bought the 120 East Exchange building that already housed the Saddle and Sirloin Club, a popular watering spot for cattlemen, ranchers, and commissioners. He opened Theo's Saddle and Sirloin Inn at the new location.

Calf fries remained on the menu.[30]

Even if immigrants had to work their fingers to the bone in Fort Worth, they found themselves much better off than in their native lands. Marcilia Bunkervich started working in Poland when she was seven years old, caring for younger children. She was paid $1 per month. The year was 1903 and Russia ruled Poland harshly, even burning the church in Bunkervich's community to the ground. Poles were not allowed to go to school, but friends sneaked Bunkervich into a Russian school for three months. Those three months were the extent of her formal education.

Bunkervich came to America at age sixteen, first obtaining a job as a housekeeper in New York. Within a year she came to Fort Worth where a brother lived, finding another housekeeping job shortly after her arrival. Bunkervich wanted to get married but was looking for a young man who was frugal. When she met Joe Riscky, also from Poland, she learned that he had saved $400 from his salary of $9 a week at Armour Packing Company. Bunkervich was sixteen when they married in 1912. To Marcilia's chagrin, Riscky extravagantly spent the entire $400 on the wedding.

Eventually the young couple had four children. In 1927, Riscky started a barbecue business which has expanded to one that caters food all over the Fort Worth-Dallas area and even occasionally out of state.[31]

In 1920, a Philadelphia Baptist seminary closed causing twenty-three of its Russian students to enroll in the Southwestern Baptist Theological Seminary on the south side of Fort Worth. Learning that several of their fellow countrymen lived on the North Side, the students wanted to convert them.[32]

The seminarians established a church in 1920 with funds provided by the state mission board, calling it the Clinton Avenue Baptist Church for Slavic People. A plain white frame structure, the building had frosted windows, oak pews, ceiling fans, a pulpit, and a baptistry. At a service on New Year's Eve, six Russian immigrants who worked in the packing plants and lived on the North Side were baptized. The young men had arrived on the North Side seven or eight years earlier, most coming without their families, with plans to work a few years and then go back with American dollars which could be traded for twice as many rubles. World War I and the Russian revolution interrupted their plans.[33]

Four young married couples, all recent immigrants, took the occasion of the 1915 wedding of Alex Bunker and Josephine Novak to pose for this picture. Standing left to right are Louise Shepelwich, Marcilia Riscky, Joe Riscky, and Joe Polinsky. Seated on either side of the bride and groom are Mrs. Shepelwich (left) and Mrs. Polinsky (courtesy Mr. and Mrs. Alex Riscky).

The parishioners became an informal community assistance group that helped others in their transition to American life. The church was the spiritual center of the Polish community, but it also provided a trilingual school of sorts, a social gathering place, and a welcome center for new immigrants. It actually did more to Americanize and indoctrinate the newcomers into Protestantism than to help them keep their old world values and traditions.

Sylvester Lozuk was one of the six young men who was baptized that first New Year's Eve in 1920. Lozuk had arrived in Fort Worth in 1913 to start a new life in America. Five years after his baptism, Lozuk replaced the first pastor, Peter Pawluk, and continued to serve the congregation for over a quarter of a century. He delivered sermons in three languages — Russian, Polish, and English — and the congregation sang hymns in Russian, Polish, and Czech from translations of the *Baptist Hymnal*. The Clinton Avenue Church remained the only Slavic Baptist Church in the entire Southern Baptist Convention for several decades.[34]

A dozen years after its establishment, the church listed a membership of sixty, but Sunday services sometimes counted 150 in attendance, including non-members and children not yet baptized. Before World War II, men sat on the right side of the aisle and women on the left according to the Eastern Orthodox custom. When Harry Polinsky, a veteran of World War II, returned home, he found that the custom of separating the sexes by a center aisle had ended.

In 1954, the Tarrant Baptist Association honored Lozuk for twenty-eight years of service. After he died in 1957, lay members continued the preaching in three languages. By 1961, however, most of the second-and third-generation congregation had moved, or had married English-speaking partners and were attending services elsewhere. The church closed its doors and the remaining members transferred to the Rosen Heights Baptist Church.[35]

By the 1920s, first- and second-generation European immigrants began to prosper. Not everyone rode the Northern Texas Traction Company's streetcars; a few bought Henry Ford's reasonably priced Model T. With more cars on the streets, service stations soon developed. Roosevelt Filling Station, located at the corner of Twenty-fifth Street and Roosevelt Avenue, opened for business on March 23, 1922. Tony Cabluck, its owner, later changed the name to Roosevelt Garage.[36]

Cabluck was born Anton Kablukov in 1873 in Grodno, Russia. As a young man, he married a girl named Olga from his hometown, and they had a daughter, Sonya. Having trouble finding work, Cabluck dreamed of a better life in America. He left his

The Clinton Avenue Baptist Church became the spiritual center of North Fort Worth's Polish community. As second- and third-generation Poles moved away from the area, however, the congregation dwindled and the wooden structure pictured above was boarded up (courtesy Johnny Cabluck).

wife and baby daughter in Grodno, telling them that he would either come back for them or send money for their passage.

After a few false starts, Cabluck found his way to Fort Worth where he got a shoe repair job in a dry goods store downtown.[37] He sent for his wife and daughter, who soon arrived. Tragically, Olga died in a fire not long after she reached Fort Worth.

Cabluck began corresponding with a young widow, Mary, from Grodno. After some time, Cabluck asked Mary to come to America with her daughter Lula and marry him. They married June 23, 1910. The new family moved to the North Side where Cabluck found another shoe repair job closer to home. Two sons, Harry and Johnny, were born in 1911 and 1914. Eventually, he purchased the lot that became Roosevelt Garage.

The business quickly became something of a magnet for local young men. They began hanging out at the Roosevelt Garage to play dominoes, moon, forty-two, and checkers, and some would use the telephone to ask their girls for a date. Others would meet there to go together to a ball game. During World War II Johnny Cabluck — who was 4-F and ineligible for the draft — functioned as a correspondent for the boys who hung around the garage. Many of his old friends wrote back from the front asking about others who once frequented the station. The queries came often enough that Johnny started a newsletter that he sent to some sixty men overseas each month.[38]

Proud of their nationalities if not their nations, the first-generation immigrants wanted to keep their cultures alive with their own churches, schools, and newspapers. Even when their respective homelands were at war with each other, the mixture of immigrants clustered together to overcome language barriers and to offer advice, and support. Often, someone would buy a paper to see what was happening in Europe, and two or three nationalities would crane their heads to read at the same time.[39] Fighting discrimination was hard enough without further antagonism among themselves.

Their children, however, wanted to speak English, become Americanized, and not be looked upon as different. Children in school often took advantage of the fact that new immigrant children could not speak English. Tony Cabluck's stepdaughter Lula later told how someone would take cookies or an apple out of her lunch. She knew who was doing it, but she could not speak English well enough to tell the teacher. Other students would laugh at her because she sounded different and did not understand what was being said.[40] Regardless, the immigrant children worked hard to get a good education because their parents had ingrained in them the value of their opportunities in America.[41]

The contrast between the broad freedoms in the democratic United States and the intolerable despotisms of eastern Europe, from which most of the immigrants had fled, gave the newcomers a great sense of appreciation for American political and social institutions. Life in North Fort Worth was difficult for first generation immigrants, but they dealt with the hardships philosophically. The immigrants "had found a country where they could work hard, save their money, and own their homes and businesses and educate their children for a better future." They could not — or would not — ask for much more.[42]

5
Energetic
Entrepreneurs

In 1889, promoters of the Fort Worth Union Stock Yards extended Main Street northward to the newly opened yards. By the turn of the century, a variety of new businesses were sprouting along both sides of the wide street.

Fifty-one-year-old Colonel Thomas Marion Thannisch, who already operated the Stockyards Inn with partner William F. Steward, did much to spark the growth of Main Street business. In 1904, he realized that investing in North Fort Worth property would be wise. He purchased a small lot on the corner of Exchange Avenue and North Main from Joe Googins's North Fort Worth Land Company. Clearing the trees away, he began constructing a two-story business building which he completed in March 1906. Thannisch opened the Stock Yards Club Saloon and Billiard Parlor on the first floor, and offered furnished rooms for rent on the second floor. Other businesses leased space from him including — at various times — a barber shop, a fruit stand and confectionery shop, an insurance firm, a real estate broker, and a restaurant.[1]

A couple of years later, Thannisch bought two adjoining lots. By March 1907 he had built a three-story brick building in which he located a restaurant, physicians' offices, a contractor, and the club bar on the first floor. He turned the entire second and third floors into hotel rooms.

In 1913, Thannisch tore the wooden structure on the first lot down and built another modern brick hotel on the land, attaching it to the building next door. He then sold the hotel to Robert Chandler who changed the name to Chandler Hotel. Though it is still referred to as the Thannisch building, through the years, the hotel has worn three other names: Planters Hotel, 1924; Stockyards Hotel, 1925-1949; Right Hotel, 1950-1982, and back to the present Stockyards Hotel after a complete renovation in the 1980s.[2]

Colonel Thannisch took an active interest in the community in which he invested, serving as an alderman of North Fort Worth for three terms. Not only did he help establish the Stock Yards Land Company which developed the 200 and 300 blocks of West Exchange Avenue, but he also invested in the North Fort Worth Ice and Cold Storage Company. Opened in January 1905, the ice plant, with a capacity of fifty tons, was welcomed by settlers moving into the area.[3]

Beside those fathered by Thannisch, many other eating establishments came and went as the bustling town grew and changed.

In the 1920s, immigrants Sarah and Hyman Applebaum, with the help of Sarah's family, started the Big Apple Restaurant at Cliff and Twenty-eighth streets. Lucille Hester worked for them, and when the Big Apple closed in the late 1950s, she opened a restaurant called Hester's on the Hill, located a few blocks west on Twenty-eighth.[4]

In 1934, two years before his graduation from high school, W. O. "Pinky" Chenault borrowed $300 and opened a drive-in restaurant on West Twenty-fifth which he called The Feed Trough. He hired the North Side High School cheerleaders as carhops, and the drive-in quickly became popular with the teenage crowd.

Chenault spent his spare time away from the restaurant learning to fly airplanes. In 1942, he joined the Army Air Force and left the restaurant to be run by his parents. He went to officer training school, soon becoming an instructor with the Air Transport Command. In World War II he flew regular missions and trained student pilots. When the war ended, he was flying cargo planes out of Love Field in Dallas. After the war Chenault started a new restaurant called Chenaults on Jacksboro Highway at Robert's Cut Off. The Feed Trough remained open until 1978.[5]

*The Thannisch Block has been standing at the corner of North
Main and Exchange for nearly eighty years. Currently the building
houses the Stockyards Hotel and the Stockyards Drug Store
(North Fort Worth Historical Society).*

In the same year that Chenault opened his second restaurant
(1946), Jesse Roach established Cattlemen's, which would soon
become a popular eating place as well as a lasting landmark. He
started out in the district with an insurance business at 2458
North Main Street, handling trucking insurance for the big eigh-
teen-wheelers that carried livestock. Roach leased a building for
his insurance business near the activity, but when the space
proved a bit large, he decided to enclose the north half and open a
little cafe for stockyards customers. He called it simply the
Cattlemen's Cafe; it seated about fifty people.

Roach hired a man to run the eatery, while he handled the
more lucrative insurance business. The man ran the cafe for about
a month but had to leave town to assist his parents whose home
had been struck by a tornado in Oklahoma. Left with no one to

manage the operation, Roach invited his niece Lois and her husband Rex Brewer to come from Beaumont to run it. They were glad to return to their North Texas home. The Brewers arrived in April 1947 and operated Cattlemen's or other restaurants for Roach for the next four decades.[6] Roach ran advertisements in national magazines and eventually gained a wide following of hungry customers.[7]

Roach wanted to build a basement, but the building owner, Ben Miron, feared that it would weaken the structure.[8] The disagreement just added to the running feud between Roach and Miron. Roach wanted to buy; Miron refused to sell. Once during the 1948 Senate race between Coke Stevenson and Lyndon B. Johnson, Miron, who favored Stevenson, was riding in a car with a friend, listening to the radio. A political announcement came on the Porter Randall show for Stevenson. Miron nodded and agreed with everything the speaker said. At the end of the announcement he heard that it had been Jesse Roach speaking. He was so upset, he got out of the car and slammed the door. Miron never did sell, but Roach later bought the building from Miron's sons.[9]

The first addition to the restaurant became the Longhorn Room at the back of the original insurance office. The second addition downstairs, adding space just north of the original cafe, had originally been a Cook's Paint Store. Roach next bought out a shoe repair shop located north of the paint store and consolidated it into the eating space. After only two or three years, the cafe became a full-fledged restaurant.

Roach maintained his insurance business until about 1980, operating it from an office in the restaurant. At various times, he started four other restaurants, and still in the 1960s found time to serve on the Fort Worth City Council.[10] Every now and then, when profits lagged, he used the income from the insurance business to bail out the restaurants.

Two other men also found their livelihoods in the North Fort Worth food industry. Both Harry D. Vinnedge and Lonnie V. (Jack) Ellis built successful food distribution companies, despite the meager resources with which they started.

Vinnedge got his start with a coffee company in Indianapolis which transferred him to Fort Worth in 1906. After a year or two,

*Chenault's Feed Trough Drive-In on West Twenty-fifth Street
featured North Side High School cheerleaders as carhops (courtesy
Johnny Cabluck).*

he borrowed $1,000 from his mother-in-law to start his own
wholesale coffee firm. Initially, he located his business across from
the Tarrant County courthouse; later he moved to Jennings
Avenue. An advertisement for the Jennings store boasted twenty
pounds of sugar for $1 and his special "Worth Blend" coffee for
twenty-five cents per pound.[11]

Moving to the North Side, Vinnedge operated Vinnedge Coffee
above a filling station on North Main for a while. In 1928, near
the eve of the disastrous decade of the thirties, Vinnedge built and
opened a new 40,000-square-foot building for his business on the
northeast corner of North Main and Twenty-first Street. It cost
$100,000 for the expansion.

Later, he brought a spur line from the railroad to his plant to
improve the distribution of his Worth Brand wholesale foods. He
also operated a fleet of trucks and employed numerous salesmen,

as well as the workers who roasted the coffee and packaged his other foods.[12]

Jack Ellis was born in Harrold, Texas, near Wichita Falls. After serving in World War I as a cook, he worked in the oil fields in West Texas and Oklahoma. In 1926, he brought his family to North Texas and began tenant farming near Avondale. Soon the family moved into Fort Worth, where Ellis worked for the Courthouse Market for a couple of years and then the grocery department of Everybody's Department Store for $5 a day[13]. He even got a job with the Works Progress Administration during the Depression hauling manure to golf courses.

Ellis's turning point came when he began working for Boldt Pecan Company delivering candy and pecans to Fort Worth grocery stores. Ellis did not know it at the time, but he had found his life's work — and that of his son and grandson too.

In 1935, when the Depression was in full swing, the son of the owner of Boldt Pecan Company came to work for his father. As a result the company laid off Ellis. Knowing that he had to do something to support his family, Ellis asked whether the owner of the Safeway Grocery Stores in Fort Worth would buy pecans from him if he started his own company. The owner agreed.

Ellis worked out of the garage behind his Rosen Heights home for the first year. Because he had to crack the pecans by hand, the entire family helped. Ellis's only son, Jackie, age fifteen in 1935, worked after school, often until midnight. Eventually Ellis began farming out unshelled nuts to non-family members and neighbors. He paid them for the shelling by the piece-work system. Ellis bought one burlap bag of nuts at a time, then gradually increased his volume.

Within a year he moved to a building on Twenty-fifth Street and invested in cracking machines. Jackie continued to work after school, sometimes until late at night during the busy season. At one of those late-night sessions, a tired Jackie became careless around the machines and cut off a finger.

Business continued to grow, and the family was able to live more comfortably. Ellis kept his delivery route, taking candy and nuts to local grocery stores and nuts to local bakeries. He stayed for five years in the building on Twenty-fifth and then moved his

Above, a truck from the Vinnedge Company ready for deliveries in the 1930s. The company distributed Worth Brand foods, coffees, teas, and spices among other products (courtesy Robert and Barty Duncan).

company to a couple of locations downtown before returning to the North Side in 1947. At that time, he purchased the present building at 1012 North Main Street from Leonard Brothers who had used it as a warehouse for their downtown department store. The Ku Klux Klan had originally constructed the building in 1925 after fire destroyed their previous auditorium. Ellis added a second floor over the old auditorium, taking advantage of its high ceiling. The slanted floors presented a problem, however, and wedges had to be inserted on one side to level any machinery.

Ellis sent Jackie to college to major in accounting. In 1955, when Ellis suffered a stroke, Jackie took over. He had already been keeping the books after his return from service in World War II. Ellis's grandson, also named Jack, joined the family business in 1983 so that he could learn the routine before his own father

retired. The little business that began in a garage behind the family home in Rosen Heights grew in a half century to one that often
grosses $10 million in sales annually.[14]

Even though most of the attention on Exchange Avenue in the
1940s was directed at beef and the booming livestock market,
some enterprising folks had discovered that the hide of a cow
could be as profitable as the meat. L. White Boot and
Saddlemaker opened for business in December 1910 at 2459
North Main Street. By 1941, the company was making the trophy
saddles that were presented at the World Championship Rodeo in
Madison Square Garden. Other rodeo associations ordered saddles
from them as well. Victor and Louis White eventually inherited
the company from their father and operated it well into its second
half-century.[15]

Frank, Silas, and O. C. Leddy, finding an old hotel on the
northwest corner of North Main and Exchange Avenue, put their
entrepreneurial spirit to work making boots. Actually, the craft
was a family tradition begun by their brother, Martin Luther
Leddy, better known to customers as simply, "'M. L." Although
M. L. never lived or worked on the North Side, he indirectly
launched the North Side store.

After losing money on a cotton crop, M. L. Leddy first operated
a shoe store, then bought out a harness and leather shop in Brady,
Texas, from an old fellow who taught him how to make boots and
saddles. During the Depression, Leddy bought up several bankrupt
shoe shops around Brady and gave them to his eight brothers to
take over. In 1936, he consolidated everything and moved to San
Angelo.

In 1941, however, Frank, Silas, and O. C. sold their interest in
the San Angelo plant back to M. L. and came to Fort Worth to
try their luck. For the first two years in the small shop on the
northwest corner of Main and Exchange streets, they turned out
nothing but boots. In 1943 they added saddlery. Then three years
later, they began selling western wear as a sideline. They turned
out forty-five pairs of handmade boots per day, making Leddy
Brothers of Fort Worth the largest handmade boot and saddle
companies in the world.[16]

The building they chose for their operation remains as much a part of North Side history as the Leddy firm. At one point in its dusty past the structure was a hotel patronized by cowboys and other travelers. Numbers can still be seen on the doors upstairs where boots and saddles are made today.

Frank Leddy proved to be a real innovator. He experimented with saddle making by attaching the fenders of a saddle with ball bearings to give easier movement and thus an easier ride. He tried making a saddle without a horn for light-weight riding, and he made a saddle for a Longhorn bull that a man rode as a publicity stunt from Fort Worth to Washington, D.C., in the 1940s.

Leddy Brothers sold their operation in 1968 to some of the family who had remained in San Angelo. Although M. L. had died in 1957, the central Texas company still operated under his name. About five years before his death, M. L. turned the operation over to his two sons and son-in-law. Then in 1981, the son-in-law, Jim Franklin, and his two sons, Wilson and Rusty, bought out M. L. Leddy's sons in San Angelo.

Wilson Franklin, grandson of M. L. Leddy, came to Fort Worth from San Angelo in 1972 at age twenty to operate the store that his three great-uncles had started thirty-one years earlier. Within a couple of decades, he had increased sales fifteen times over. Of the dozen or so companies that fashion true handmade boots today, Leddy's sells the largest volume. It seems only fitting that this famous name in western boots continues to craft the product on the North Side.[17]

Roland Ecelon Lewis also started his career by first working for his brother. An early Fort Worth businessmen, he came from Minnesota to Texas in the 1870s. At first, he worked for the Texas and Pacific Railroad, drilling water wells across West Texas ahead of the construction crews. After marrying a Fort Worth girl, Lewis went to Salt Lake City, Utah, to work in a furniture store but returned to Texas a few months later to work in his brother's furniture store. In the next two years, Lewis opened three of his own furniture stores which he eventually combined into one store in the 2300 block of North Main.

Lewis settled his growing family on Hemphill Street south of downtown. Each morning he caught a streetcar near his house and rode it to his store north of the city. He maintained his interest in his North Side furniture store until his death in 1940 at age eighty-five. His descendants later moved the store three blocks farther north and across the street where a fourth generation still runs the business.[18]

Another enterprising North Side entrepreneur was Clarence Marshall whose crippled arm and leg did not prevent him from operating a newsstand in the 100 block of West Exchange in front of Lewis Drug Store. His stand consisted of racks hung on the wall of the building and covered with a canvas awning. The electric street-car stopped there and later the bus, so passengers could buy a paper while waiting for their ride. For many years, rain or shine, in hot or cold weather, Marshall stood under his awning handing out newspapers. In the early 1950s, he moved inside and operated a bookstore.[19]

Many of those folks congregating on the North Side to buy and sell cattle or to work in the packing houses needed the services of a barber. The Stockyards Barber Shop, owned by Lewis Lawrence, employed six full time barbers and even provided several showers and tubs for baths. A rancher could come in with new clothes he just bought from the Jacobsons or Jake Greines or bring clean ones from home and spruce up before getting a good meal and a bed for the night. Lawrence supplied soap and towels for twenty-five cents. His prices for other services were: shave, twenty cents; hair cut, twenty-five cents; and shampoo, twenty-five cents.[20]

Foy Babb began a barber shop in the stockyards area in 1924 and renamed it B & B Barber Shop in 1946 when Jack Bridwell joined him in business. They kept working until 1984 when both retired and they closed the shop.[21]

Although he would lend his name and talents to the growth of North Side business in a completely different venue, cattle interests brought seventeen-year-old Samuel David Shannon to Fort Worth on Christmas Eve in 1883. Arriving by train in Fort Worth after selling his horse and saddle in Bowie, Texas, where he had worked for a short time as a cowboy, Shannon wandered the streets of downtown Fort Worth looking for employment. Instead of a job, however, he found two saloons to every block. In one of these establishments he got into a poker game and lost. When he walked out of the saloon, he only had thirty-five cents in his pocket, not enough to get a room in a hotel for the night.

Shannon walked back to the train station at the south end of town and spent the night on a bench there. He spent twenty-five cents for a breakfast of ham and eggs. Then he set out to start his new life with just ten cents in his pocket. Shannon walked the mile up Main Street to the courthouse asking at least fifty different people for a job. No one obliged.

A fellow near the courthouse finally told him: "I heard that the Palace Livery Stable needs a man." Shannon hurried to the livery stable and soon got a job rubbing down horses for owners George L. Gause and John Wilkes.[22]

Either Wilkes or Gause arranged for Shannon to eat a meal at a cafe nearby on his first day of currying horses. One of them told him he could sleep in the hayloft at night and cover up with a horse blanket. Shannon worked at the livery stable for eight months, starting at five in the morning and working until nine at night, seven days a week. He earned $35 per month.

Fortunately for Shannon, life in a frontier community was full of opportunity for anyone willing to work hard. He first changed his sleeping arrangements, then his job — both for the better — obtaining a room in a boarding house for $3.50 per week. He found a job at a mattress factory at $36 per month, but he only had to work six days a week. He even began to save some money.

One Sunday, Shannon went for dinner to the home of one of the young men he had met at the mattress factory, Will Cummings. Shannon met Will's sister, a young widow named Marie, and they were married in 1893. Shannon tried several jobs to support his family, one of them as a meat market proprietor, but the store burned in 1906. After that tragedy, he approached his former boss at the livery stable, George L. Gause, and worked out a deal to create a funeral home on the North Side. The partners rented a part of the Rosen Inn on North Main near Meyer Greines's store and next to an Owl Drug Store operated by Homer Kendrick.[23]

Shannon and Gause started the North Fort Worth Undertaking Company, their initial investment consisting of a horse and buggy, office furniture, four adult caskets, and mortuary equipment. The business grew to the present Shannon's Funeral Home at Twelfth and North Main and various other insurance, funeral, and cemetery investments. Shannon's fourth-generation descendants still participate in the operations. Shannon himself turned to politics in his later years, serving as Tarrant County's tax assessor-collector, as a justice of the peace, a state representative, and as county judge.[24]

One type of business that began to boom in both Fort Worth and the North Side in the 1920s and 1930s was used cars sales. Cattlemen from West Texas would sell a carload of animals at the yards and then go shopping for a car before heading back to the ranch or farm. Also, Fort Worth at that time was fast becoming a wholesale market for used cars. Dealers from all over West Texas would come to Fort Worth to buy automobiles and take them to their home towns to resell them.[25] The expanded market gave some of the entrepreneurs on the North Side an idea: send some folks up to Dearborn, Michigan, to buy good used cars from the Ford Motor Company.[26]

Sellers and Wiley at 800 North Main were the pioneers and leaders in the wholesale used car business in Fort Worth. Eugene Sellers, known as "Bud," and Dick Wiley owned the company. Sellers acted as buyer and seller, while Wiley ran the office and handled the finances.[27]

Other used car lots on North Main in the 1930s belonged to Johnny Shrasek, Ray Wills, Brady Young, and Norman Phillips. The men played checkers, poker, dice, and so on to wile away the time between sales. They hired young fellows like Esmond Scarborough to wash and polish the cars to a sparkling shine which would attract customers.

Since used cars were never guaranteed, if one wanted to be safe, one bought a new vehicle.[28] In the 1930s, two new-car dealerships existed in North Fort Worth — Bradley Burks Ford at 2204 North Main, and Cliff Magers Chevrolet at Twenty-third and North Main. In 1933, Cliff Magers sold more trucks than any other dealer in the state of Texas.[29]

In 1926, W. T. Hobbs began building truck trailers at 600 North Main to capitalize on the need for cattle-hauling equipment. Although he sold out to M. J. Neeley in 1932, the company has continued under the name Hobbs Trailers.[30]

A young man from Tennessee named A. M. Pate had no idea

that he would come to Fort Worth and eventually begin a business that would become worldwide. Pate sold oil and roof coating for a Cleveland, Ohio, company before World War I, spending many hours traveling by horse and buggy on company business. When some of his bosses moved to a Dallas firm just before World War I, Pate moved too. In Dallas he became a salesman for the Oriental Oil Company, where he became friends with Carl Wollner, the credit manager for the company.

When World War I erupted, Pate enlisted in the armed forces. Although Wollner was a citizen of the U.S., his German ancestry caused him problems and he left his job with the Dallas firm to come to Fort Worth and enter the stock brokerage business until after the war.

When Pate returned from overseas, Wollner suggested that the two men start a business together similar to the one for which they had both worked in Dallas. Wollner would run the office and Pate could handle the sales in the field. Pate mulled over Wollner's proposition. He had just gotten married in Tennessee on his way home from the war in Europe, and he felt the financial necessity to accept his old job back with Oriental Oil. The two men continued to visit back and forth with Wollner urging Pate to start up the new company, but Pate kept putting him off. Soon a baby came along, A. M. Pate, Jr., to complicate Pate's decision. Finally, in September, 1922, Wollner and Pate started their company and hired three other employees with $1,500. They called the firm Panther Oil and Grease Manufacturing Company, capitalizing on Fort Worth's nickname, "Panther City."[31]

In the years that followed, Pate hocked his wife's engagement ring two or three times to make payroll. When out-of-town salesmen came to Fort Worth to report, they slept at the Pate house to save hotel expenses.

"I remember seeing my father give salesmen the spare tire off his own car or an overcoat off his own back to keep them going," remembered A. M. "Aggie" Pate, Jr., many years later.[32]

Pate and Wollner located the company's first plant in a building just a couple of blocks east of the old M. G. Ellis School in the 1500 block of North Main. In 1928, they constructed a block-square factory at about the 800 block of North Main. Their business had expanded to twenty-eight states by that time. In the 1930s, Pate moved his family to El Paso to develop the Pacific Northwest and Mexico as customers.

Carl Wollner died suddenly in 1945, so the senior Pate bought Wollner's shares of stock from his heirs, making him the sole owner of the business. Unfortunately, Pate died in 1947. His son, A. M., Jr., who had been working for the company nine years, took control upon his father's death and remained president until his own death in 1988, when Aggie's brother Sebert took over as chairman of the board.

After more than sixty years of expansion, Texas Refinery Corporation, as it is now called, produces many different petroleum related products and employs a worldwide sales organization numbering in the thousands. Five separate corporations exist under the umbrella of the parent corporation with offices in Texas, Canada, Luxembourg, and Mexico.

6
On the
Wild Side

Crime and carousing in the bars on Exchange Avenue became so common in the first half of the twentieth century that people far and wide heard of Fort Worth's wild reputation. In fact, *Fort Worth Press* columnist Jack Gordon once told the story about an Arkansas writer named Spider Rowland who came to Texas and wrote: "I have finally discovered the difference between Fort Worth and Dallas. Folks in Dallas want to know WHAT you have, but in Fort Worth they ask, "What'll you have?"[1]

In the bars along Exchange Avenue, that question outnumbered all others. The livestock market and the meat-packing plants on the east end of Exchange Avenue were definitely a man's world. Few women accompanied their husbands to sell cattle, hogs or sheep. The wealthy ranchers who did bring their wives along left them in hotels in downtown Fort Worth with money to shop at stores such as Monnig's, Meacham's, W. C. Stripling's, and Sanger Brothers. Even the few female stockyards office employees, who later worked for the numerous commission companies in the Exchange Building, hesitated to walk along Exchange Avenue unescorted.

If the stockyards area was rough, it was also exciting. Just how rough and tough is illustrated by the legend that Depression-era hoodlums Bonnie and Clyde stayed at one of the hotels in the area. The present-day Stockyards Hotel at 109 E. Exchange Avenue presents the Bonnie and Clyde story as one of its featured attractions. The hotel does not know the exact room Bonnie and Clyde occupied (and cannot prove that they ever did), but legend claims that it was on the third floor overlooking the corner of North Main and Exchange, a strategic location that would allow the desperadoes to see everyone coming up and down both streets. The hotel currently maintains a "Bonnie and Clyde Suite" in that spot.

Exchange Avenue certainly attracted more than its fair share of crime. Thirty-year-old Nathan Monroe Martin entered the Stockyards National Bank on Exchange Avenue just west of the coliseum about noon on Saturday, August 9, 1930, carrying a satchel containing a bottle of nitroglycerin. He intended to relieve the bank of $10,000 of its "excess" cash without causing a particular stir. Yet much more than a "stir" resulted. Martin walked up to the first open teller's window he came to; behind it sat Fred L. Pelton. Martin issued his request which the bank president also overheard. Before Martin could conclude his withdrawal, police rushed in the front door of the bank, having received a frantic telephone call from the bank president. He had requested, however, that the police not enter the building but apprehend the robber after he left. The unexpected arrival of the police so unnerved Martin that he dropped his satchel. The nitroglycerin inside exploded, killing the would-be robber and Pelton, the bank teller. Two other persons suffered injuries as well.

Witnesses claimed that one could hear the blast a half-mile away. Trees around the building lost leaves from the force of the explosion. Bank furniture, money, light fixtures, and other move-ables were scattered throughout the bank lobby. The bank's official owner, the Fort Worth Stock Yards Company, immediately put men to work around the clock repairing the $3,000 in damages. They finished in time for the bank to open as usual on Monday morning.[2]

Incidents like this one were a far cry from the Wild West days when a gang of desperadoes rode into town, cleaned out the bank, and galloped off in a cloud of dust and probably a hail of bullets. Reality on Exchange Avenue even differed from Depression-era gangsters like Bonnie and Clyde who blasted their way into banks with machine guns and got away in fast Fords.

Another attempted robbery of the Stock Yards National Bank

in the 1930s came closer to a different popular image: the old Keystone Kops. Four men in a big, black car drove up to the bank and parked. Three of them got out and went inside, leaving the fourth to keep watch. Meanwhile, a delivery man from the pharmacy on the northeast corner of Main and Exchange emerged from the drugstore and climbed on his three-wheel motorcycle to make a delivery. When he cranked the cycle to start up the motor, it popped loudly and backfired several times. The nervous robber keeping guard assumed that the drugstore delivery man was a policeman and that the noise was gunshots. He quickly hailed his friends before they could finish their "business" with the bank. The would-be robbers hurriedly scrambled into their car, knocked out the rear window so that they could shoot at any pursuers, and began firing wildly. A bystander had the presence of mind to approach a real policeman standing on a nearby corner and tell him what was happening.

"But I can't leave my post," he cried. "I have no car."

A woman offered her car.

"But I can't drive!" he argued.

"I'll drive," the woman assured him.

With that, the policeman and female chauffeur began chasing the crooks north on Main Street toward Saginaw. The robbers had planned their strategy well (except for the possibility of a backfiring motorcycle), for they carried a sack of nails or tacks in the backseat. They scattered the sharp objects behind the car as they roared down the street so that anyone following would get a flat tire. Several spectators along Main Street jumped in their own vehicles and gave chase, but these high-minded citizens soon found themselves with flat tires and gave up. The would-be robbers made a successful getaway, and North Side drivers were still having flats a week later.[3]

Exchange Avenue was not the only rambunctious street in North Fort Worth. On Samuels Avenue, where enthusiasts had earlier built the city's first race track, two-story structures hid a small red-light district. This "petit" district carried no particular name but served the north side of the river and stayed out of the headlines, while its more notorious cousin on the south end of town, "Hell's Half Acre," became the subject of numerous stories and legends.

Samuels Avenue, named for Baldwin L. Samuels, whose farm lay at the end of it, originated as a north-south road from the farm into Fort Worth. Samuels had been a genuine "forty-niner," amassing a fortune of some $40,000 within a few months of his arrival at the California diggings. Unfortunately, on the night before he intended to take a steamer home, robbers stole all his money. The never-say-die Samuels returned to his claim, worked extra hard, and a few months later left with $15,000. He first purchased a farm in Kentucky and later moved to Texas.[4]

North Siders and other Fort Worth folk visited Grunewald's Park and Dance Pavilion on Samuels Avenue from 1885 to 1905, although some church-going residents disapproved of the wild dancing and carousing. Peter Grunewald operated the park and dance pavilion, a large wooden hall with shuttered windows and seats around an oval floor. A saloon usually did a booming business in the basement.[5] Mule cars ran north on Samuels to the park; as one car turned around at Samuels to go downtown to Front Street (now Lancaster), the other car would turn at Belknap and go back to Grunewald Park.[6]

Samuels Avenue's wild reputation was later improved by two civic-minded ladies, Belle Burchfield and Delia Collins. During Fort Worth's wide open saloon days, the ladies frequently assisted a Methodist minister on errands of mercy in Hell's Half Acre and the North Side red-light district. A truly enlightened woman, Mrs. Burchfield talked the Tarrant County commissioners into buying a house of ill repute to use as an orphanage for the children of the "fallen" women they had been assisting.[7]

The two women assembled a distinguished board of trustees for their orphanage and began converting the house into a suitable home for the children. The organization later incorporated as the Fort Worth Benevolent Home Association. At a February 1903 meeting of directors, the newly elected officers included Khleber M. Van Zandt, president; George Q. McGown, vice-president; E. L. Huffman, treasurer; and Alfred W. Samuels, secretary. Later a benefactor donated land for a new home, and the directors made plans for its construction. Arnold Park, created in the 1950s and named for Major Ripley A. Arnold, who established Fort Worth, now stands on the site of the first house.[8]

*Typical of the old mansions that once graced Samuels Avenue is
the William Garvey house at 769 Samuels (North Fort Worth
Historical Society).*

In December 1921, a packing plant strike not only created major labor violence for the second time in Fort Worth's history, but also contributed to Niles City's annexation by Fort Worth.[9] The nationwide strike involved 45,000 packing house workers in fifteen states, with many plants shutting down entirely. On the North Side, however, Armour and Swift managed to keep their slaughter lines moving because many men crossed the picket lines. Violence erupted as active strikers halted the scabs and tried to prevent them from reaching the plants.

Fred Rouse, a thirty-five-year-old black man, continued to work each day at the Swift plant. As he left work on December 6, 1921, a large group of angry strikers accosted him. Rouse, frightened by the daily harassment, had hidden a .32 caliber pistol on his person. When the crowd surrounded him, he pulled out the gun and fired twice. He hit two young brothers, Tracey and Tom Maclin, striking the former in the leg and the latter in the chest.

Niles City police immediately arrested Rouse, but a mob took control and beat him into unconsciousness. Officials placed him in City-County Hospital in Fort Worth (later renamed John Peter Smith Hospital) and set a guard nearby. One evening six days later, when Rouse was beginning to recover, the policeman outside his basement room became complacent and careless. When he stepped away from the door, about thirty men entered the hospital room wearing masks and forcibly took Rouse from his bed. The next morning police found his bullet-riddled body swaying limply from a tree near North Twelfth Street on the road from Samuels Avenue to the packing plants.[10]

The Ku Klux Klan of post-Civil War days reappeared nationally during the 1920s. Organized violence at that time usually meant the Ku Klux Klan, and the hanging of Fred Rouse was probably Klan-inspired. This would explain the masks and the lack of any identifiable suspects. The thirty men who killed Fred Rouse and got away with it, if not actual Klansmen, used Klan tactics to rid the community of a black man who had dared to challenge a collective will.

The Klan originated east of the Mississippi in Pulaski, Tennessee, after the Civil War. The combined efforts of a shocked citizenry and federal power eventually stamped out most Klan activity during Reconstruction, but it was just sleeping, not dead, at the close of the nineteenth century. A new Klan burst forth, reborn at Stone Mountain, Georgia, in 1915, appealing to the native-born, white, Anglo-Saxon, Protestant, anti-alcohol, and largely rural factions in America. Much of the population in North Texas in general and North Fort Worth in particular fit those characteristics, except for the small neighborhood of immigrants. The Klan's chief targets, nationwide and locally, were the predominately Catholic immigrants from central and southern Europe, who arrived in the U.S. after the beginning of the twentieth century.[11]

Because of their different backgrounds and heritages, these new immigrants did not share the conservative Protestant aversion to alcohol. In addition, they competed for factory jobs in the booming industrial areas. The large packing plants of the North Side, employing four or five thousand workers, drew many of these foreigners.[12] Thus the North Side became ripe for typical Klan activity — men dressing up in pillow cases and bed sheets, trying to terrorize and intimidate those who seemed different.

One Klan incident stirred a great deal of excitement in late May 1922 when an initiation ceremony was held on a hillside "several miles northeast of the city and about three-fourths of a mile from a public road."[13] North Side residents suspected that something unusual might happen when about dusk one Friday night a parade of six hundred cars began heading out North Main Street. Citizens in several North Side neighborhoods miles away could see a huge burning cross about thirty feet tall and with arms extending fifteen feet in width. The ceremony began at 9 P.M.

Curious onlookers who followed the caravan to see what was happening couldn't get within a half mile of the meeting place because Klan guards spread out to surround the initiation site and yelled, "Move on." That night 3,000 men in full robe and hood stood in the light of the burning cross, while 932 new members took the oath of allegiance to the "Invisible Empire" and became Knights of the Fort Worth Klan No. 101.[14]

Klansmen touted the event as the initiation of one of the largest new classes in the country, certainly the next to largest ever sworn in in Texas.[15] Cars began leaving the scene about midnight, the guards leaving last.[16]

Although ostensibly a "secret" organization, the Klan became so accepted in Fort Worth in the early 1920s that it constructed a large auditorium at 1006 North Main Street for regular meetings and programs. The Klan made no attempt to disguise the purpose or owners of the structure; residents openly knew it as the Ku Klux Klan Meeting Hall.

Perhaps the location and activities became a bit too well known for a supposedly secret organization. Early on Thursday morning, November 6, 1924, residents in the general area of the Klan hall heard fire sirens and saw flames shooting high into the air. Witnesses told police they noticed an automobile leave the building a few minutes before someone turned in the first fire alarm. As the fire roared out of control and reached the height of its flames, witnesses also heard an explosion that someone described as a "muffled roar." The conflagration spread so rapidly that a hamburger stand south of the Klan hall also caught fire and burned to the ground. Traffic on North Main Street halted for nearly an hour as firemen blocked the street and onlookers stopped to watch. Early workers on their way to their packing house jobs waited impatiently as the streetcars halted for fear that debris might fall on them if they passed in front of the building.[17]

Two hours after the fire began, only "four charred crumbling walls" remained of the Klan hall. Ironically, after the fire had been extinguished, a sign depicting a fiery cross still stood in front of the building. Officials declared the Klan structure a total loss, with the estimated damage being $70,000. Authorities immediately suspected arson.

That same day, the Klan offered a $500 reward for information leading to the arrest of the person or persons who had set the fire. Even while the ruins smoldered, Klan members began talking of rebuilding, replacing their destroyed meeting hall with an even "greater and costlier" structure. Eventually the Klan succeeded in constructing a large hall adjacent to the site of the one they lost.

More immediate matters faced the Klan leaders, however. On the Wednesday evening before the fire, members had been practicing for a minstrel show set for the following Friday and Saturday nights, to which they had already sold a large number of tickets. The destroyed building had a seating capacity of 4,000 and was one of the best Klan halls in the country, according to the "Cyclops" who headed the local chapter.[18] The fire left the Klan with no place to stage their show and not much time to locate an alternate site.

A solution to the dilemma came from an unusual source. J. Frank Norris, a nationally known preacher of the First Baptist Church in Fort Worth, sent a telegram from Houston where he was holding a revival meeting and offered the auditorium of his church for the Klan's minstrel show.

"I am 100 percent for fair play," he said. "Let the Klan have the auditorium over all engagements."[19]

Norris' magnanimous gesture backfired as soon as the church announced it because, in point of fact, another group already had booked the church auditorium for that same Friday night, a ladies music club called the Euterpeans. The ladies refused to step aside for the Klan because they had already sold 2,000 tickets to their own function. But the ladies did more than just say "No." They filed a court injunction on Friday afternoon, November 7, to prevent the Klan from having its minstrel show at the church hall. The music club presented its contract for that Friday night and for three other nights.

The Klan offered more money for the auditorium than the women were paying, and the church needed the money, but a contract was a contract. When the court ruled in the ladies' favor, the Klan pressured them to withdraw, but they again refused. The Euterpean ladies assured the Klan that they were not "anti-Klan"; in fact, some of their own members most likely were Klan members, too, they said.[20]

The Chamber of Commerce resolved the problem when they let the Klan hold the minstrel show in their downtown building. After the show, Klan leaders began looking for a new site to house their headquarters while their own building was under construction. They carried on business as usual from a temporary office downtown.[21]

The well-known Klan meeting hall fire became a part of North Side lore. Folks told stories that the fire actually started when a pilot dropped a bomb from an airplane as he flew over the KKK building that Wednesday night. Authorities never found the guilty person or persons, whether it was an aviator-arsonist or someone on the ground making a getaway in an automobile. The episode remains one of the fascinating mysteries in the history of the North Side.[22]

The next year, KKK officials dedicated the large brick auditorium they had constructed at 1012 North Main Street. They called their meeting place the North Main Street Klavern. A stage originally stood at the east end; an exterior, narrow, three-story section once housed the curtain which could be raised or lowered as needed. Seats rested on a slight incline. The modern structure no doubt impressed many who viewed the meeting hall; yet time was passing the Klan by. The "Invisible Empire" declined in the late 1920s for a number of reasons, not the least of which was a state law in 1926 which made the wearing of masks in public a felony.[23]

When older North Siders remember the wildness around the stockyards, they don't generally think of stockyards bank robberies or KKK activities. Mostly, they remember the madams and prostitutes operating out of sleazy, run-down Exchange Avenue hotels, bookies and gamblers taking bets on horse races set at Arlington Downs, or bootleggers delivering illegal whiskey in brown paper bags. These were the kinds of "normal" activities that everybody called "wild" during the 1920s and 1930s. What perhaps average citizens only heard rumors about and guessed at were the dope rings, car bombings, and antics of real hoodlums. These activities took place too, and just whispers of their reality could frighten honest citizens into silence.

Jokester Bob Vance, who worked at Brady Young's Used Car Lot in the 2100 block of North Main, took advantage of the general fear of criminals to play a harmless trick. Young's lot was located next door to Johnny Shrasek's car lot. Vance and his fellow workers could easily see through Shrasek's office window as he dealt with customers or talked on the telephone. One day, two men drove into Young's lot looking for a good, fast car. Vance waited on them, but Young's lot didn't have the kind of car they wanted. Vance took them next door because Shrasek had a new 1933 V-8 Ford.

The two strangers traded in their Model-A Ford and unloaded

their personal belongings from the Model-A to the new V-8.[24] They transferred a shotgun, a rifle, and two hand guns to the V-8.

After the men left, Shrasek paid Vance a commission for the sale, their usual practice. After Vance got back to Young's office, he decided to have a little fun. He called Shrasek and told him that the two men who had just bought the V-8 were dangerous bank robbers. About an hour later he called back, disguising his voice, and told Shrasek that he was the man who had just bought the new V-8. He said the car had thrown a piston rod through the motor block and that Shrasek had misrepresented the car. He was on his way back to kill him.[25]

Vance could look next door and see Shrasek talking on the telephone. As soon as the conversation ended, Shrasek ran out of the office, jumped in his car, and left. He never came back that day. Even the following morning when he returned, he remained nervous. Finally, someone told him that Vance had played a joke on him.[26]

With bank robbers and bootleggers, petty con artists found a place on the North Side. Some North Siders remember crooks who promoted oil leases all over West Texas. They composed a convincing letter and prospectus and then paid Brown and Morrow Multigraphing Company to run off a lot of copies. The confidence men blanketed the area with the promotional literature, took the money out of the letters that responded, and threw away the rest.[27]

Legitimate but frowned on by the church-going citizens on the North Side was the Idle Hour Club, a pool and domino parlor owned and operated in the 1920s and 1930s by Swede Burkitt and his wife Birdie on Exchange Avenue near the Maverick Hotel and Bar.[28] Another establishment, the Blue Moon Ballroom, operated in the basement of the old post office building on Twenty-fourth next door to the Llano Hotel. The Blue Moon became a popular place for the ranchers and cowboys because girls, called "taxi dancers," would dance with the fellows for ten cents a dance. As the recording industry emerged, bars began offering juke boxes. The owners would find a small space for a dance floor and hire the "taxi girls" to keep the festivities going and coins flowing into the music machines.[29]

While alcohol remained illegal, "speakeasies" emerged. After the repeal of Prohibition in 1933, folks called these places — the Wagon Wheel, Rodeo Bar, Jimmy Seay's, and the Blue Bonnet Club on North Main Street — that sold beer and permitted dancing, "honky tonks."

Some tell the tale that when the ten-foot wall of water gushed down Exchange Avenue during the 1942 flood, a drunk staggered out of a bar and saw it coming. He rushed back inside to warn everyone, but no one believed him. Patrons were drenched in their scramble to escape after the water struck.[30]

Certainly, floods and drunks were the mildest activity of the wild life on the North Side during the several decades that North Main Street and Exchange Avenue represented the center of the city's shady shenanigans.

7
Tamer Family Fare

Just a few blocks away from the bars and brawls in the stockyards, families went about their lives, going to church on Sunday, sitting out in their yards on summer evenings talking to neighbors, and taking the kids to Marine Park for free movies on Saturday nights.[1] Children walked to school. In the afternoons, young girls played jacks or paper dolls that they made themselves from Montgomery Ward or Sears-Roebuck catalogues. Boys played baseball or took part in activities at the North Fort Worth Boys' Club. Some paid nine cents at the New Isis Theatre to see either a cowboy serial show or Hollywood's latest release.

In the early days, water wagons and meat markets made deliveries. So did ice houses, dairies, bakeries, and numerous other businesses. All in all, it was pretty tame family fare.

Most of the first settlers of the North Side were churchgoers. Revivalism had swept the South in the first half of the nineteenth century, making the South — including Texas — a part of the so-called "Bible Belt." Citizens organized the first community church service in the one-room frame Marine schoolhouse which M. G. Ellis had built. W. H. Rowland, a Confederate veteran and Baptist minister, rode on horseback from Azle, a small community northwest of Fort Worth, to preach at this first service sometime in 1888. Several religious groups shared the school with the Baptists.

The Baptists were the first denomination on the North Side to construct their own building for worship services. Mr. and Mrs.

Louis C. Haywood called a meeting of Baptists in the area on April 20, 1890, and informed them that her uncle, M. G. Ellis, had donated property at Fourteenth and North Jones streets on which to construct a building. The Baptists met at that site for approximately five years, then at Ross Avenue and Twenty-third streets for eight years. In 1903, the congregation moved to Fifteenth Street and Circle Park Boulevard and called themselves the Boulevard Baptist Church until 1925, when the members changed the name to North Fort Worth Baptist Church. They met in that location until 1985, when the congregation moved to a large facility on Interstate-35 north of Loop 820.[2]

James T. Bussey, the county missionary for the Tarrant Baptist Association, saw the summer of 1906 approaching and knew that hot weather meant revival time. People liked to get outdoors where it was less stuffy, and they did not mind hearing some fire and brimstone at the same time.

Bussey got started early that spring. In April 1906, he arranged to borrow a tent from the Tarrant Baptist Association, purchased the previous fall for just such work. He found a vacant lot in the

The Fort Worth Boys Club, built in 1937, at Ellis Avenue pro-vided a place for activities for a membership of 2,000 annually (courtesy Robert and Barty Duncan).

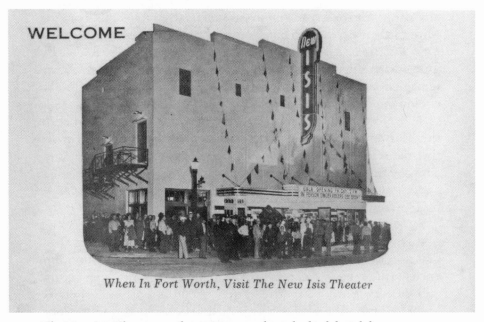

When In Fort Worth, Visit The New Isis Theater

The New Isis Theater — the management hosted a birthday club and sent out birthday greetings to local kids who could redeem them for a free pass to the movies (courtesy Robert and Barty Duncan).

2400 block of Columbus Avenue and recruited some help in erecting the tent.

Dr. Charles W. Daniel, pastor of the First Baptist Church in downtown Fort Worth, agreed to come up to North Fort Worth to speak at the services. At the end of the revival, the handful of respondents agreed to meet again the last Sunday in April to establish a new church which would be called the Rosen Heights Baptist Church. Eighteen persons met that Sunday, and seven more soon joined them. These first twenty-five charter members along with the growing congregation eventually obtained a lot in the 2500 block of Roosevelt Street and constructed a frame building that cost $175.[3]

A serious illness in 1921 turned a young lawyer named Jesse Garrett into a preacher who would influence the Rosen Heights Baptist Church with his enthusiasm and personality more than any other person in the many decades after its establishment. Most of the early preachers served the congregation only a year or two. But in 1925, when Jesse Garrett arrived from Rockdale, Texas, with his wife and two children, he found a home. Garrett remained almost thirty-two years at Rosen Heights Baptist, influencing the congregation and the community in many ways.[4]

The North Side Church of Christ also began its existence in the Marine schoolhouse in 1899, when M. H. Moore preached the first sermon to twelve people and became the regular pastor.[5] The congregation erected their first building at Fourteenth Street and Circle Park Boulevard in 1903. The parishioners moved to their present location at 2001 Lincoln in 1949.[6]

A new Catholic parish was a direct outgrowth of the packing plants. Several of the officials who had moved down from Chicago were Catholic, and they added their considerable influence and numbers to the many Catholic immigrants from central and eastern Europe. In the spring of 1902, Father Joseph A. Campbell from the Dallas-Fort Worth Diocese held the first local mass north of the Trinity River in the home of Mr. and Mrs. H. A. Mulholland at 1305 North Commerce. The Catholic Church then organized a parish north of the Trinity, the second in the Fort Worth area.[7] Reverend M. A. McKeough, the first appointed priest of the new parish, served until 1905.

In 1903, the parish constructed its first frame church building on North Houston Street (then called Lake Avenue).[8] In part, funds were raised by Mrs. Mulholland who donated a vacant lot on Berry Street in south Fort Worth; the lot was raffled off for $2,000 which went toward the new building. The North Fort Worth church, called All Saints Catholic Church, moved to its present location at 214 Northwest Twentieth Street in 1952.[9]

Presbyterians, the Christian Church, Methodists, and Episcopalians also organized churches in the early days of the North Side. Members of the North Fort Worth Presbyterian Church, organized in 1903, constructed a wooden building at 1500 Clinton Avenue in 1905.[10] Rosen Heights Presbyterian Church began in 1928 with sixty-six members meeting in a rented store building at 1520 Northwest Twenty-fifth Street.[11] Chestnut

The North Fort Worth Baptist Church in 1915 (North Fort Worth Baptist Church).

Avenue Christian Church, later the North Fort Worth Christian Church, originated in 1909.[12]

North Fort Worth Methodist began in 1899 from the union of the two earlier congregations of the Marine and Little Fossil Methodist churches. In 1907, the congregation changed its name to Boulevard Methodist Episcopal Church South. They constructed a two-story brick church building in 1927 at 1600 Circle Park Boulevard.[13]

Sundays after church, families liked to picnic outdoors. One of the oldest parks in the entire city of Fort Worth is Marine Park, located at Twentieth Street and Ellis Avenue. Civic-minded residents of the Marine community organized the outdoor facility about 1894, building a nine-foot picket fence around it. Apparently, builders wanted the fence to keep out stray cattle and other "critters," for very few people lived in the area at that time.[14]

A small branch of Marine Creek running through the park was dammed to create a two-acre lake. The entire park covered fourteen acres.[15] Over the next two decades, people protested so much about the lake attracting mosquitoes that city officials finally had it drained.

In 1909, when Fort Worth incorporated the North Side, the Fort Worth Park Department included Marine Park in its jurisdiction. Officials supervised play in the summer for children, including baseball games, sandbox play, and yo-yo contests. Someone built a green wooden bandstand, and live concerts became a highlight of the summer season. Sometimes there would be readers, singers, dancers, harmonica players, fancy trick ropers, and jugglers. The park department invited students from the Dockery School of Oratory, the Losh School of Music, and the Burgess School of Dancing to perform.[16] Sometimes there were even community sing-alongs.

Old-timers remember an artesian well in Marine Park. A pipe stood thirty-five to forty feet tall, and water gushed out in spurts, the excess running off in a drainage ditch under Ellis Avenue.[17] It no doubt provided cool, refreshing relief to park patrons on hot summer days.

Then in August, 1926 a swimming pool was opened.[18]

During the Depression years, Leonard Brothers Department Store in downtown Fort Worth showed free movies in most city parks, including Marine Park. A large truck would arrive with a movie screen set up on the back. The department store furnished cold drinks, popcorn, and snow cones. During the movie, advertisements highlighted Leonards' specials.[19]

Summertime was not the only season in which citizens enjoyed gathering in Marine Park. During Christmas, families gathered around a large Christmas tree to sing carols.

Marine Park was not was not alone in entertaining North Siders. In 1905, on opening day of Sam Rosen's amusement park, White City, twelve thousand people entered the gates on a hill near Grayson and West Twenty-fourth streets in Rosen Heights. Rosen brought in merry-go-rounds and Punch-and-Judy shows, created an artificial lake, and built a dance pavilion.[20] The story is told that Sam Rosen built White City after a visit to Chicago where an amusement park intrigued him. He constructed his local version near the end of his streetcar line to increase use of the streetcar; White City was a real showplace for the entire city, not just the North Side. Rosen added a small steam train that ran on tracks around the park and a "Tunnel of Love" boat ride. He even built a White City Hotel near the park.[21]

Some North Side youngsters tasted their first ice cream cones at White City. Oliver Shannon, son of Dave Shannon, said that he and his friends ate the ice cream and threw away the cone because they weren't sure it was edible.[22]

The park at White City also featured a baseball diamond — the largest in the county at the time — a grandstand, a theater, and an amusement area with a Ferris wheel. It even boasted one of the nation's first calliopes which filled the air with carnival music.[23]

Through the years, interest in the park declined and its various entertainments closed. As people moved into the area and constructed homes, the older structures were dismantled.

Unfortunately, on June 17, 1933, a fire broke out in the last remaining building — a dance pavilion — at the White City resort. Owners had only recently renamed the building the Hackberry Grove Dance Hall and had just hosted a dance. Fire marshals said the fire was probably caused by a cigarette.[24]

Closer to the stockyards area, before Colonel Thannisch developed the west end of Exchange Avenue, the avenue boasted a place frequently used for carnival-type events. Sometimes medicine shows would set up tents and wagons on the vacant lots there. People generally did not mind listening to a sales pitch for a useless patent medicine if they could also enjoy a free puppet show or similar entertainment. One of the medicine shows featured a huge redwood tree ten or twelve feet in diameter which had been hollowed out and placed on a large wagon. Inside, the show owner displayed some trinkets and artifacts from the frontier, such as Indian headdresses. He would only let those people who had bought a bottle of the patent medicine go inside the redwood tree. The medicines were cure-all tonics consisting mostly of alcohol and food coloring. Apart from producing a little "buzz," they probably did not hurt anyone — but neither did they help. Congress passed the first Pure Food and Drug Act in 1906, partly to regulate the less scrupulous dispensers of patent medicines.

One of the owners of a medicine show who came frequently to the vacant hill at the end of West Exchange Avenue in the first decade of the twentieth century must have been an awfully poor salesman. He often borrowed money from the local banks just to keep his activities going. His show, with its several tents of talented performers, required a large payroll. In one tent he featured a new gimmick called a "moving picture show." A boy turned a crank which made the pictures move when projected onto a screen in the darkened tent. But when the owner of the medicine show could not pay his note at the bank, he lost his entire operation to North Side banker Louis Tidball. The year was about 1912, a time when the West began outgrowing the old medicine shows, just as it would abandon vaudeville a few years later.[25]

Needing to earn back the money tied up in the unpaid loan, Tidball scouted around for someone to help run the part of the show he thought still had some profitable life left in it. He finally decided that the moving pictures might be the most crowd-pleasing part and rented a building on West Exchange in which to exhibit them. He hired a young man named John H. Sparks, Jr., to turn the crank. Images projected on the screen represented the ultimate in silent movie enjoyment of the day. Sometimes — when nature intervened — patrons of the silent show heard sound effects. One night they accidently got a true-to-life soundtrack when a thunderstorm erupted outside at the same time as a thunderstorm flashed on screen.

Eventually Tidball decided to form a company to show the moving pictures. He sold stock in the newly created North Fort Worth Amusement Company. In 1913, after raising $15,000 in financing, Tidball constructed a building on North Main to show the pictures, calling it the Isis Theatre. Many movie houses at that time used similar exotic names and far-eastern decor. The ornate building featured a piano and an organ to provide accompaniment for the silent movies. Thunderstorms stayed outside. Tidball hired only four employees in 1913.[26]

When the building burned in 1935, the amusement company

constructed a second theater at a cost of $29,800 and called it the New Isis.[27] The theater, which seated 920 movie-goers, opened March 27, 1936, on the same ground in the 2300 block of North Main Street on which the old Isis had stood. To celebrate its first birthday, the New Isis served an angel food cake — weighing over 1,000 pounds — that almost reached the ceiling of the lobby.[28]

In April 1942, flood waters rose five feet inside the theater. The next day when people came to see the damage, management showed them a free movie.

Tidball operated another theater on the North Side, the Roseland, at 1438-1440 North Main Street. When it first opened in 1920, John H. Sparks, Jr., managed it. By 1929, Tidball took over, renaming it the Rose Theater. By 1945, the name had changed to Marine Theater, and Lee A. Burkhalter managed it.[29]

Possibly because the North Side was the factory part of town with a large number of poorly educated workers earning low wages, poverty was a problem. Children wandered the streets and seemed at loose ends if both parents worked. A Fort Worth crime report for 1934 showed that the North Side had the highest concentration of juvenile delinquents in the city, mostly Anglo boys. After this report became public, civic-minded Elizabeth DeCory Vaughn called about twenty women together on January 10, 1935, to do something about it. She and her daughter, Hazel Vaughn Leigh, had been active with the Panther Boys Club in Fort Worth since its inception in 1928. They left the Fort Worth club to form one for the boys of the North Side.

Leigh went to Dr. Abe Greines, president of the North Fort Worth Kiwanis Club, to ask for help with their plans. The men in the Kiwanis Club pledged to find a place for the North Side boys and to provide medical care for those who needed it. Mrs. Leigh wanted reading and art to be taught as well as boxing and basketball.

The North Fort Worth Boys Club opened on February 1, 1935, with 205 boys meeting in the Boulevard Methodist Church gymnasium. By September 10, 1937, the club moved into its own building at Twentieth Street and Ellis Avenue.[30] The building was debt free by July 1940, mainly because many North Side citizens had donated free materials and labor for the initial construction.

The original one-story brick, box-shaped structure cost $25,000. It contained a playroom with various table games, a library with 1,400 volumes, a well-equipped gymnasium, and a workshop where boys could learn woodcraft. The boys made toys, book ends, and other serviceable articles such as shelves and simple small tables. In the beginning, the club did not serve meals, but frequently someone donated food to the boys, so a kitchen in the building proved useful during those times. The youngsters played softball, tennis, and other games on an outdoor playground.

The purpose of the club from the very beginning was "to provide recreation and constructive training" for boys, especially those whose parents could not provide it. The club also oversaw medical attention donated by physicians and collected clothing for poorer children. Club sponsors helped older boys find work.

Fortunately, in the early years, two generous doctors practiced medicine in offices across the street. Abe Greines and Russell Calkins, a dentist, provided free services to the boys.

Boys ages six through fourteen could come to the club each day after school from 3:00 to 6:00 P.M.[31] Mrs. Vaughn, Mrs. Leigh, and others were gratified that juvenile delinquency in the area dropped seventy-five percent the first year that the boys club operated. Mrs. Leigh became executive director and remained active until 1973. At one time, the national boys club movement recognized Mrs. Leigh as the only woman who had ever been executive director of a boys' club. She remained prominent in the boys' club movement in Tarrant County for nearly half a century.[32]

The North Fort Worth Boys Club merged with the Panther Boys Club in January 1990. The name changed to Boys and Girls Clubs of Greater Fort Worth with six locations throughout the city. The club on Twentieth and Ellis Avenue on the North Side remains active, still serving meals during the summer.[33]

One of the establishments that became popular for family fun in the late 1930s was Pullman's Skateland, at 541 North Main Street. W. B. Pullman designed and built one of the largest roller skating rinks in the state in 1938 at a cost of $16,000. Roller skating had become a national pastime — almost as popular as baseball — and like baseball it provided a family activity in which everyone could participate. In fact, at Pullman's Skateland 500 people could skate to music at the same time on the 9,000 square feet of hardwood floor.

Steel girders supported an arched roof over the 70-by-150 foot open-sided skating rink. In those days, before refrigerated air conditioning, the open air aspect made the structure cooler than if it had been enclosed. During World War II, Pullman sold the rink, and later owners bricked in the building and put on a roof. The children of North Side residents enjoyed skating there until the 1950s.

Another popular group activity, especially in the 1930s, was the Dance Marathon, held in a big building covering nearly half a block at the corner of North Main and Grand. The building originally served as a livery stable, blacksmith shop, and carriage house. At the dances, a blind man played the piano and would take any request. Sometimes couples danced for days before a contest ended, but they stayed with it to win whatever prize was offered. Those who wanted to watch paid ten cents admission and cheered the couple of their choice.[34]

The fat stock show, organized at the stockyards in the early days, also provided exciting family enjoyment each year. After the first show in 1896, the stockyards company agreed to host an annual show if cattlemen would cooperate. Cooperate they did. Over a decade after the first show, cattlemen helped raise $50,000 to demonstrate their good faith; they would continue participating if the Fort Worth Stock Yards Company would construct a coliseum. In 1908 the North Side Coliseum opened. In the new facility that same year, officials hosted the first cutting-horse contest held under electric lights.

One of the most exciting events of the stock show on the North Side, officially called the National Feeders and Breeders Show, came on the crisp spring morning of Tuesday, March 14, 1911. Five thousand persons gathered early in the three-year-old Coliseum. Questions buzzed through the audience. The man causing all the excitement, ex-Rough Rider and former President Theodore "Teddy" Roosevelt, was scheduled to speak at 9:00 A.M. As the crowd in the coliseum awaited him, other spectators lined both sides of North Main Street to watch as he passed by in a parade.

The coliseum became the site of the first indoor rodeo in 1918.
This photo was taken about 1920 (North Fort Worth Historical
Society).

When Roosevelt arrived at 7:30 A.M. in his special train at the Texas and Pacific Railroad station, veteran Rough Riders joined the military guard standing at stiff attention. Roosevelt was carried by car to the Westbrook Hotel for a cowboy breakfast with host Colonel Samuel Burk Burnett, who was then president of the show. After breakfast, the parade escorted Roosevelt out to the stockyards. The former president's car moved north on Main Street behind a detachment of mounted police and a military band as assembled crowds greeted him.[35]

Roland Lewis, a staunch Republican and owner of Lewis Furniture and Stoves in the 2300 block of North Main Street, asked his wife to bring the children out to the store to watch the president's entourage go by. Mrs. Lewis, a Democrat from an old southern family, at first refused. Later, after her husband went to work, she relented and loaded her six children and even some neighbor youngsters on the streetcar to ride to the North Side store. After she arrived, Lewis got out some little red chairs from

his store and lined them up along Main Street. President
Roosevelt, who had a large family of his own, loved children.
When his car rolled adjacent to the furniture store, he saw the
row of children in their little chairs.

"Delighted, delighted," he said, standing and bowing in their
direction. Mrs. Lewis reportedly felt more kindly toward Roosevelt
after that and referred to him as "our President" which she had
refused to do before.[36]

At the yards, Roosevelt's visit was upstaged somewhat when a
huge fire started in the feed barns about 7:00 A.M. and swept
through six acres of stables of the horse and mule barns. A number of prize-winning horses, gathered for the stock show, perished
in the blaze. Some mules, sheep, and hogs also died.

Crowds gathered to watch the fire and the tall pillar of smoke
which lost itself in the low-hanging clouds. Then they stood
around waiting for Roosevelt to appear, while hoping that the
occasional drops of rainfall would not drench them.[37]

The crowd inside the coliseum cheered heartily as Teddy
stepped out on the stage. Just after Roosevelt took his seat on the
platform, Colonel Burnett rose to quiet the crowd in preparation
for the ex-president's speech. Fort Worth Mayor W. D. Davis halted Colonel Burnett with the announcement that something
important must take place first. An old fellow on crutches, accompanied by three of his children, struggled to the stage. He was
Charlie Buckholtz of San Angelo who had served as Roosevelt's
cook with the Rough Riders during the Spanish-American War.
The old soldier mounted the stage by the side of his former chief
and the crowd applauded as the two men clasped hands.
Buckholtz told his former chief that his application for a pension
had met a snag in government red tape. Roosevelt took down the
number of his claim and the circumstances and promised to con-
tact Washington immediately.[38]

Then Roosevelt took center stage and thanked the mayor for
the opportunity to speak. "I jumped at the chance to come to Fort
Worth in the first place because of Fort Worth and in the second
place because the invitation came through some old and valued
friends. Besides having done various other things with them while
President, I went with them on a wolf hunt once. And one of the

finest spectacles I ever saw was Burk Burnett taking the late lieu-
tenant general of the United States Army in a buckboard over an
out back after a coyote. I tell you; it would have made an eastern-
er's eye bulge."[39]

Roosevelt could not resist his usual advice to a crowd: "Develop
the right kind of citizenship, especially here in Texas, the state which
will have so great a part to play in the future of the republic."[40]

Outside the coliseum the rain held off and the firemen fought
the blaze in the horse and mule barns, but the fire completely
destroyed the wooden structures. The next year stockyards owners
constructed modern brick horse and mules barns which still
remain.

Stock show promoters changed the name to Southwestern
Exposition and Fat Stock Show in 1917 and added an indoor
rodeo in 1918, reputed to be the first indoor rodeo in the world.
About the same time, promoters began the custom of crowning a
queen on opening night. Many a young North Side girl dreamed
about being chosen for the honor, and numerous girls from the
more prominent families entered the competition. The queen and
her court of beautiful young ladies, who added a touch of glamour
to opening night festivities, posed for many photos and attracted
much interest from shy and not-so-shy cowboys.[41]

The show continued to meet every year in the heart of the
stockyards district until 1942. With an accompanying carnival, it
occupied the same ground every year just west of the coliseum.
Because several of the exhibit buildings were serving as assembly
plants for war production, producers cancelled the show in 1943.
Gasoline rationing also made it difficult for people to come any
distance to attend the event. When the show resumed in 1944,
officials still could not use the exhibit buildings. Therefore, they
held the event in the Will Rogers Complex which the city of Fort
Worth had constructed in 1936 on the west side of Fort Worth.[42]
The stock show never moved back to the North Side, a development that old-timers still resent but cannot change. The show
immediately proved successful at the spacious new location, and
promoters still refuse to tamper with it. In fact, the annual
Southwestern Exposition and Livestock Show remains Fort
Worth's single most lucrative event.

The stock show promoters' decision not to move back to the North Side after World War II might have been reinforced by those who recalled the Trinity River flood of 1942 which covered some of the North Side, including the floor of the North Side Coliseum. All the mud and dirt had to be removed before the building could be used again. The task of cleaning it fell to R. G. McElyea, who rented the coliseum the next year from the city of Fort Worth, which had owned it since 1936. McElyea spent $75,000 to put the building back in shape. He added a hardwood floor so that he could have dances and then brought in big name bands from all over the country. For many years, he scheduled country-western music in the coliseum on Saturday nights, wrestling on Monday nights, and various other activities during the week. He leased it for conventions, trade shows, and even a basketball tournament. It did not stand empty if McElyea could find an event looking for a space.[43]

Elvis Presley provided one of the more interesting shows that McElyea brought to the North Side Coliseum during the more than thirty years that he and his family leased it. In 1956, when Elvis had just begun to emerge as a new rock star, McElyea signed Presley and his band for $500 for a future performance that year. Elvis' popularity rose before he made his Fort Worth appearance because another of his hit records had reached the top of the charts. Presley and his current manager wanted more money for the booking, but McElyea held him to the $500 price. Later, of course, several of Elvis' hits drove his asking price into the stratosphere. After he became a star of Hollywood and Las Vegas, neither Elvis nor his manager, Colonel Tom Parker, would have considered such a booking. The story is told that the low fee gave Elvis such a bad feeling that he would not consider returning to play in Fort Worth for many years. In fact, sixteen years elapsed before he returned to the city for sell-out performances in the downtown Convention Center. But North Siders and R. G. McElyea could boast that they hosted the legendary "King of Rock and Roll" when he was still just a pretender, before he was crowned.

McElyea died in 1964, but his daughter, Elizabeth Moore, operated the coliseum until the mid-1970s. At that time, Steve Murrin obtained the lease from the city and brought rodeo back to the North Side for the first time since 1942. He held eight seasons of a fall and spring rodeo circuit before 1983, when he suspended them because of renovation plans for the city-owned coliseum. In 1986, the newly renovated structure was declared a historical landmark in a ceremony with appropriate speeches and festivities by the mayor, the officials of the North Fort Worth Historical Society, and local historians. Rodeo returned in the summer of 1988, sponsored by the city.

From movies in the park to movies at the New Isis, from medicine shows to White City amusements, from the self-improvement of attendance at church or the boys club, North Siders have always had a variety of entertainment available to them. Unlike the brawls and robberies on Exchange Avenue and in the red-light districts, these activities pulled the community together, adding to North Side's civic pride.

8

Transportation Revolution

If the stockyards were the lifeblood of the North Side, the various modes of transportation were the veins. Each development in road and transport design meant more cattle could be brought to the pens. Even when the stockyards were no longer the largest industry in Fort Worth, transportation loomed large.

In the early days of Fort Worth, the most heavily used route between downtown and North Fort Worth crossed the river northwest of the bluff at a low-water crossing. When the river was high, folks took a ferry. From that point, the road curved eastward to Birdville, Grapevine, and Dallas. In 1888, the city and county decided to build a bridge across the Trinity on what would become North Main Street just north of the county courthouse. Completed the following year, the two-lane wire suspension bridge with retaining walls and two sidewalks cost taxpayers $10,250.

By 1900, increased activity had made the two-lane bridge inadequate, but city officials refused to act. The situation worsened after Armour and Swift opened for business in 1903, causing the population of North Fort Worth to boom. By 1910, the many vehicles crossing the old iron bridge to downtown created frustrating traffic jams. At that time, Fort Worth planned to build four bridges to connect the center of the city with outlying areas. Intending to make the North Main Street viaduct the largest, city officials wanted it to be wide enough for two vehicles and two electric streetcars to pass at the same time. Engineers designed two eight-foot-wide walkways as well.

The completed structure would eventually bear the name of Buckley B. Paddock. Paddock, editor of the *Fort Worth Democrat* for many years, had editorially urged building the stockyards, meat-packing facilities, and railroad lines. He had also served as mayor of Fort Worth for four terms and secretary of the Board of Trade, forerunner of the Chamber of Commerce.

Though born in Cleveland, Ohio, in 1844, Paddock grew up in Wisconsin. His mother died when he was five, and he spent his boyhood on the frontier, working in lumber camps and sometimes living with Indians. He had little schooling. When the Civil War erupted, Paddock surprisingly joined a Confederate cavalry regiment, soon rising to the rank of captain. After the war, he married a southern girl and settled in Fayette, Mississippi, where he studied law, passed the bar exam, and practiced for several years.[1]

As a young man of twenty-eight, Paddock came from Mississippi on horseback across Texas in 1872 to find a community in which to settle. He left his wife and family back home, planning to bring them westward when he found a suitable place. On the road, he met former Texas governor J. W. Throckmorton, who suggested Fort Worth as a town of promise for an ambitious young family man. Throckmorton suggested that Paddock call on Major Khleber Van Zandt when he got to Fort Worth. Van Zandt, who had been running a newspaper only because the community needed one, immediately turned the operation over to Paddock.

Paddock eventually purchased the newspaper, taking on the triple role of publisher, editor, and chief reporter and using the *Fort Worth Democrat* to promote the growth of the city.[2] In the spring of 1884, Paddock gave up active newspaper work, but he kept a financial interest in publishing. He later became a historian for the city and a commentator about Fort Worth in general, still promoting the city at every opportunity. He was, for example, the prime mover behind the 1889 project to construct a Spring Palace agricultural exhibit south of downtown, and his efforts brought visitors to Fort Worth from all over the country. Paddock feuded for years with Dallas newspapers about the relative merits and demerits of the two rival cities. Indeed, his efforts fueled a rivalry that would continue into the twentieth century. Paddock also served one term in the state legislature from 1912 to 1913.

Although he was engaged in investments and securities (rather than his newspaper) when he retired at age sixty-five, Paddock had been a civic booster of Fort Worth for nearly forty years.[3]

It seemed only fitting that Paddock's eventual monument be a structure of modern engineering that served a practical purpose. The bridge was the first concrete arch in the United States built with self-supporting reinforcing steel. It would be one of only a few bridges in the world with its weight resting solely on ball and socket joints. These joints at the feet and crown of each of the four sets of parallel supporting arches allowed the bridge to rise and fall as temperature changes caused contraction and expansion of the arches. The bridge was an engineering marvel of its day.[4]

During construction, a committee of citizens presented a request to the Commissioners Court to name the viaduct after Paddock.

"He has been a potential factor in the upbuilding of this city from its early beginning and in the development of Tarrant County for more than a third of a century," the committee report stated. "No man in Texas has lived a more unselfish life or has contributed more of his time, energy, and substance to the public welfare. His chief delight is to be of service to his fellow men."[5]

The Commissioners Court did not deliberate long before complying with the citizens' request. The new bridge crossing the Trinity at North Main Street was named Paddock Viaduct.

Although Paddock never lived on the North Side, his editorials which urged creation of a livestock market in Fort Worth and his support for bringing the packing houses accomplished much to promote the North Side. In fact, as early as 1875, Paddock had suggested that a packing plant be built in Fort Worth: "There is no reason why Fort Worth should not become the great cattle center of Texas," he wrote.[6]

When the $400,000 bridge opened in July 1914, it accommodated two vehicles and two streetcars abreast just as its designers had envisioned. Crowds of people came from all over the city, especially from the North Side, to view the opening ceremonies. Today, Paddock Viaduct is still the principal link between down-

Paddock Viaduct, Fort Worth, Texas.

The Paddock Viaduct shortly after construction — it has been renovated a number of times since this postcard was made and remains the primary artery between downtown Fort Worth and the North Side (courtesy Robert and Barty Duncan).

town Fort Worth and the North Side. It is one-third mile long (1,752 feet) and rises ninety-nine feet above the Trinity River.[7]

In the second decade of the twentieth century, oil discoveries west of Fort Worth greatly expanded city business activity. West Texans had always considered "Cowtown" the place to buy and sell cattle and agricultural products; now it was the place to have oil refined. In fact, when Niles City enlarged its boundaries in 1922, in an attempt to prevent annexation by the city of Fort Worth, a Gulf Oil Company refinery and pipeline plant was included in the jurisdiction of the little community. The Gulf Refinery, built in 1912, boasted a daily capacity of 8,000 barrels of oil.[8] Other refineries on the North Side included Magnolia, Marathon, Pierce, Premier, Sinclair, and White Eagle. By 1927, seven Fort Worth refineries were producing 85,000 barrels of crude oil daily.[9]

The oil companies often tapped into reserves of natural gas from the earth as they drilled. In 1917, Lone Star Gas Company discovered a significant supply of helium in its natural gas pipeline which ran from Petrolia Field near Wichita Falls to Fort Worth. Consequently, the U.S. government built the world's first helium production plant in North Fort Worth on Blue Mound Road; the plant opened the next year during World War I.[10]

Plant workers extracted the helium from the natural gas, then returned the gas to a collection station for Lone Star's customers to use.

During early wartime experiments, an eight-foot fence of expensive, knot-free lumber surrounded the plant to prevent "peeping Toms" from witnessing any activities inside. Because the nation was at war, soldiers under the command of Z. W. Wick guarded the facilities around the clock. The North Side plant supplied all the helium gas used in Army and Navy lighter-than-air ships (dirigibles).[11]

After the war, the United States government spent over a million dollars producing helium in two experimental production plants at the same North Side location: the Linde Company and the Air Reduction Company. The government estimated that the helium extracted by the plants was worth between $250 and $400 million at pre-war prices.[12] The president of the Fort Worth Chamber of Commerce, Ireland Hampton, gave credit to Fort Worth Congressman Fritz Lanham for bringing the plant to North Fort Worth.[13]

World War I ended before any locally produced helium could reach Europe for use in dirigibles, but two of the U.S. Navy's dirigibles, the *Shenandoah* and the *Los Angeles*, could be seen moored at the helium plant in the early 1920s. These impressive-looking giants of the air were part of the Navy's early experiments with air power. Fort Worthians felt fortunate to be able to get a glimpse of the lighter-than-air craft.

A few years after it visited Fort Worth, the *Los Angeles* was broken up for scrap. The fate of the *Shenandoah* was considerably grimmer. In September 1925, she was caught in a thunderstorm in

Ohio, tossed about the skies, and broken into three parts, crashing to the ground and carrying the commander and fourteen of the forty-nine crew members to their deaths.

Partly as a result of the crash of the *Shenandoah* and other lighter-than-air ships, the U.S. Navy began winding down its experiment with dirigibles. In 1926, it stopped supervising the two Fort Worth plants and turned supervision over to the Bureau of Mines, a part of the Commerce Department.

The plants closed for good in 1929. Afterward, the U.S. Army used the facilities for its Airways Division Office, later the Civil Aeronautics Authority, and ultimately the Federal Aviation Agency.

While a lighter-than-air industry only briefly got off the ground in Fort Worth, conventional fixed-wing aircraft facilities found a ready home in "the city that cows built." Fort Worth businessmen, especially Mayor H. C. Meacham, worked hard in the early 1920s to acquire a municipal airport north of the city. On May 23, 1925, a 170-acre open field called Fort Worth Airport opened on North Main Street just four-and-one-half miles from of the courthouse.[14] It was known later as Meacham Field.

The story of Meacham Field cannot be told without including the life and career of William G. Fuller, who took his first airplane flight as a youngster in 1911, only eight years after Wilbur and Orville Wright made their famous flight. Fuller's father paid $25 in Trenton, New Jersey, so young Bill could fly as a passenger. The youngster already enjoyed building model airplanes and entering them in the New Jersey State Fair.[15]

Fuller's second flight came in 1912 — in a dirigible. Two years later he got a job in New Brunswick, New Jersey, with an aviation engine manufacturer. Then in 1916, he joined the Army Signal Corps, trained as a pilot, and became one of the first enlisted men to achieve pilot status in World War I. During the war, the army ordered Fuller to oversee assembly and flight of the first four planes ever to fly from Love Field near Dallas.

After the war, when the government, through the Federal Model Airway System, set up airfields coast to coast, Fuller came to Fort Worth to look after the city's airport-in-a-pasture. At the time it boasted only a twelve-by-twelve building for tools and supplies. The city assumed control from the Army on April 1, 1926.[16] When Fuller's army enlistment expired in 1927, he became airport manager of the new field he had almost single-handedly created from the North Side pasture. He served as airport manager until his retirement September 1, 1961.[17]

The United States Army was the first principal user of the field. In 1927, promoters changed the name to Meacham Field in honor of the man who had urged its creation. Not only was Meacham instrumental in placing the field under municipal supervision and ownership, but he also personally headed the finance campaign to obtain donations for the initial landscaping and beautification project.[18]

By 1927, several private airlines operated out of Meacham Field — Swallows, Travelaires, Fokkers, and Ryans. That same year the first passenger on an out-of-state flight arrived at Meacham Field: Bill Fuller's wife arrived on a Texas Air Transport flight.[19]

Excitement ran high on the North Side on Monday, September 27, 1927, when America's most famous airman, Charles Lindbergh, was scheduled to land at Meacham Field. He was making a series of cross-country appearances following his famous solo flight from New York to Paris just weeks earlier. Fuller, who had served with Lindbergh at Brooks Field in San Antonio, planned to be the first to greet the young hero and help him move his airplane into a stockade built to protect it.[20]

"Lucky Lindy" buzzed Fort Worth about two in the afternoon, and then circled Meacham Field in *The Spirit of St. Louis* three times before landing. When the tall, slender young aviator crawled out of the monoplane, a large crowd broke into cheers. Governor Dan Moody and a host of state, federal, and city officials greeted him when he stepped to the ground.[21]

Dignitaries rode with Lindbergh in a parade down North Main Street to Panther Park, the baseball field close to downtown. There a crowd of 30,000 school children awaited Lindbergh. A twenty-five-piece band from the 144th Infantry Regiment played John Philip Sousa's "Stars and Stripes Forever" and then led the parade to downtown Fort Worth. Later that night, Lindbergh was the guest of honor at a civic banquet in the Hotel Texas downtown.[22]

In the late 1920s, mail and small freight arrived at Meacham

At top, Fort Worth Municipal Airport, 1927 (North Fort Worth
Historical Society). Below, an early view of the airport, later
named Meacham Field (courtesy Robert and Barty Duncan).

Field. Airmail pilots flew open cockpit planes and faced freezing temperatures during the wintertime. When the winter of 1928-1929 proved exceptionally cold, the pilots packed their helmets and clothes with newspapers to provide more warmth. Frequently, workers on the ground had to lift the pilots in and out of their planes because of the bulky paper padding.

Meacham Field has been the scene of several "firsts" or record-setting events. Fuller's hand in publicizing the field could be seen in the background of all these activities. In 1928, Earl Akin piloted from Meacham the first glider in the world ever towed by another aircraft.[23]

Two young men from Meacham Field set another aviation record in 1929. "Reg" Robbins and Jim "Cowboy" Kelly attempted a new flight endurance record. With the donated money and equipment of their sponsors, Robbins and Kelly reconditioned the *Fort Worth*, a commercial plane, for the endurance attempt. Robbins, an auto mechanic who had been flying only a short while, served as pilot, and Kelly, a West Texas cowboy who a year earlier had only dreamed of being a pilot, was co-pilot and mechanic.[24]

Kelly's tasks included climbing out on the catwalk of the airplane three or four times each day to grease the rocker arms which opened and closed the valves. A refueling aircraft owned by Midland Oil Company provided gasoline periodically, dropping a seventy-five foot hose which Kelly would grasp and insert into the tank.

The flight began at 11:53 A.M. on Sunday, May 19. The two men knew they would have to stay airborne until at least 7:13 P.M. on Saturday, May 25, to break the record of 150 hours, forty minutes, and sixteen seconds set by an Army Fokker aircraft.[25]

Unfortunately, Robbins became nauseated after about twenty-four hours in the air. He sent a note down asking Fuller to "send me some medicine tonight."[26] The refueling plane could do this.

The flyers circled Meacham Field several times on Monday, the second day of the flight, but they remained out of sight to onlookers most of the time. The two men took turns sleeping in a Navy hammock which swung in a cramped place over the airplane's auxiliary gasoline tank. Fuller kept floodlights and a beacon burning at the field all night to help the pilots orient themselves. Following refueling on Monday, the auxiliary plane lowered a sack containing two bottles of hot coffee, a bottle of water, ham sandwiches, fruit, and newspapers. Hopefully, Robbins also received the needed medicine.[27]

Excitement mounted on the ground as the days passed and the "boys" remained in the air four, five, six, and finally seven full days. They stayed airborne for four hours into the eighth day, making the total 172 hours, thirty-two minutes and one second before landing at Meacham Field. As the tired airmen crawled out of their airplane, a cheering crowd threw armloads of flowers over their heads.[28] The two men gained international attention for their feat in the *Fort Worth*, and many compared their accomplishment to Lindbergh's trans-Atlantic flight two years earlier. Telegrams poured in with contract offers ranging from appearances in vaudeville shows to aeronautical jobs.[29]

The municipal air field on the North Side has remained important. The weather bureau established a station there in 1930 that still operates. By the mid-1930s, Meacham Field provided commercial flights to both east and west coasts. Flying time to either coast was ten to twelve hours, but the trip generally took longer because the planes landed a couple of times. Depending on layover time, the trip could even take three days because commercial airplanes did not fly at night if they could avoid it. In the 1930s, the airport ranked third in the nation in handling of mail, passengers, and freight.[30] Wiley Post, Amelia Earhart, Wilmer L. Stultz, and other famous flyers landed at Meacham Field in the 1920s and 1930s. Other celebrities arriving there included Humphrey Bogart, Robert Taylor, Bob Hope, and Will Rogers.[31]

During World War II, Braniff and American airlines operated a total of thirty-four flights a day from Meacham. Delta also operated from the field. Following the war, airport activity declined because Amon G. Carter and his associates had built Amon Carter Field east of the city. Love Field in Dallas then took over most of the major commercial flights, outstripping Carter's renamed Greater Southwest International Airport. In 1973, Dallas-Fort Worth International Airport swallowed up Greater Southwest and took most of Love Field's trade as well. In recent

Fort Worth Mayor Van Zandt Jarvis (fourth from left) and Amon Carter (third from right) participate in the ceremonies for the opening of American Airlines at Meacham Field (North Fort Worth Historical Society).

years, Fort Worth Meacham Airport, as it is now officially named, has continued to see heavy use both as a private and a public airport, and has been especially important in training student pilots.[32] Would-be pilots come from all over the world for flight training because Fort Worth's weather allows them to log flying hours much faster than many other locations.[33]

In the center of the Meacham Field terminal lobby, a large stuffed steer called "Old Timer" stood for many years. He came from a herd of Texas longhorns belonging to Amon G. Carter's Shady Oaks Farm west of Fort Worth. Carter donated the steer to Meacham Field when the airport dedicated a plaque to him which read "Dedicated To the Matchless Texan Amon G. Carter, Range Rider of the Air, In Appreciation of His Effective Activity in the Advancement of Aviation Throughout the World. June 19, 1937."[34] Carter, a pioneer of the business side of aviation, bought into a small southern airline in the early days of the industry and helped turn it into the giant carrier known today as American Airlines. Ironically, it was the construction of the airport named after Carter east of Fort Worth that drew air traffic away from Meacham.[35]

Growing up near Meacham Field and watching all the airplanes arriving and departing may have sparked an interest in flying for one North Side boy: Horace Carswell, Jr. Carswell, whose father Horace, Sr., worked at Swift for four decades, graduated from North Side High School and attended Texas A & M University. When World War II erupted, he joined the service and flew airplanes in the Burma-India Theater. He was killed in action when he sank a Japanese cruiser and his plane sustained direct hits in the process. Carswell kept the plane going until crew members could bail out. While trying to reach land with an injured crew member who could not jump, Carswell crashed into a mountain near the China coast. Young Carswell, who had reached the rank of major, was posthumously awarded the Congressional Medal of Honor. Following the war, Fort Worth named its own military air base in his honor and reburied him on its grounds.[36] When Carswell Air Force Base closed recently, Carswell's remains were moved to Oakwood Cemetery and a memorial service honored him on March 19, 1993.[37]

From railroads, to oil refining and aeronautics, Fort Worth has played a large part in developing transportation for the country. Even more specifically, the North Side has had a leading role and at one point took center stage.

9
From Conquering Cats to Praying Colonels

Football and baseball have long been the favorite sports of most North Siders, although a bit of fast running on the track has sparked some interest too. Baseball overshadowed everything, however, as the major employers, Armour and Swift, fielded their own teams. More important, though, was the reign of the team that served as the mascot for the entire city, the Fort Worth Panthers, known popularly as the Cats.

Baseball caught on early with Fort Worth citizens, although some of the first games were not held on the North Side. Members of a local baseball club met at the courthouse on March 10, 1877, and decided on the none too colorful name — Fort Worth Baseball Club.[1] When the team, already called the Cats by 1879, traveled to Houston to play the Buffs, they went by buckboard. It took a week.[2] And it was not long before sports fans in the larger Texas cities formed the Texas State League on January 4, 1889, with teams in six cities: Galveston, Houston, Waco, Fort Worth, Austin, and Dallas. Rumor has it that some teams got mad and quit the league before the first season ended.[3] No matter, shortly after the turn of the century the Fort Worth nine was well established and newspaper writers nicknamed them the "Panthers," for the "Panther City."

In 1911, the new owner of the Fort Worth Cats, J. Walter Morris, decided to move the baseball team from Haynes Park on East Lancaster, Fort Worth's southeast side, to a new location.[4]

Morris had been doing it all — playing, managing, and handling the team's business arrangements. That proved to be too much, so he brought in a friend, Paul LaGrave, to help him. They built a new 5,000-seat ballpark costing $35,000 two blocks west of North Main Street on North Seventh Street. At first they called it Morris Park but later renamed it Panther Park.

Streetcars ran a block away on North Main Street. Conductors would hold cars ready for the end of the game so people could board immediately.[5] Morris used several incentives to boost attendance at his new facility. He became the first owner of the Cats to attach rain checks to tickets. Keeping Panther Park clean, discouraging profanity, and working to make the fans comfortable helped attract women to games.[6] It was probably Morris who arranged for the Fort Worth municipal band of twenty members to accompany the Panthers on out-of-town trips during winning seasons.[7]

Jacob Atz managed the Fort Worth team while it played at Panther Park, and the local boys dominated the Texas State League from 1920 through 1925, winning the championship six times in a row. In 1923, the Cats sent nine players to the American League Detroit Tigers. Such big-leaguers as "Pee Wee" Tavener, "Topper" Rigney, "Lil" Stoner, August Johns, Joe Pate, Larry Woodall, Jimmy Walkup, "Goldie" Rapp, Les Mallon, "Lion" Chagnon, and Clarence Kraft received their early baseball training under the leadership of Jake Atz and the managers who followed him.

One story told by old-timers is that Jake Atz's real last name was Zimmerman, which always made him last in line for everything. To alter that, when he went into the service during World War I, he simply changed his name to Atz.[8] Sportswriters called the team Atzmen. By 1925, reporters called Atz's team the "Conquering Cats" because they reigned as the undisputed baseball champions of the southern conference, going on to win five Dixie League pennants in the six years they won the Texas League, losing only in 1922.[9]

One of the most talented Cats players in the conquering days was left-handed pitcher Joe Pate, hero of a generation of Cats' fans in the Atz era. Pate started his sports career pitching baseballs

Left to right: Will Stripling, Paul LaGrave, major leaguer Rogers Hornsby, Doak Roberts, and J. Walter Norris in 1923 (courtesy Flem Hall).

and playing quarterback in football at Fort Worth's Central High School. His family had moved to Fort Worth in 1897 when Pate was three.[10]

Just out of high school, Pate broke into professional baseball in the spring of 1912 with the Dallas Giants. When he won four and lost six, they sent him to Texarkana where he won twenty-seven and lost six, leading the league and winning the pennant. In 1915, he played in the Nebraska State League and then abandoned baseball to join the army during World War I. In 1918, Pate joined the Fort Worth Cats. He became the only pitcher who twice won thirty games — in 1924 and 1931 — in the Texas League. Pate's tally as the Cat's pitcher was 176 victories and 51 losses from 1918 to 1925.[11]

Pate could be mistaken for a ham actor on the mound with his flamboyant mannerisms; he never got in a hurry or got excited.

He practiced psychology on the batters with long delays between pitches and a delayed windup.

After his career with the Cats, Pate pitched for teams in Philadelphia, Minnesota, Birmingham, Shreveport, and New York. He became an umpire in 1933.[12]

LaGrave Field was completed in 1926, at a cost of $160,000, and the Cats occupied it that same year. Located on the corner of Northeast Seventh and North Jones streets, three-quarters of a mile north of the courthouse, it stood three blocks east of the old Panther Park. Officials named the new baseball park in honor of Paul LaGrave, a prominent businessman who had worked with J. Walter Morris to build Panther Park. LaGrave served as business manager of the team from 1916 until shortly before his death in 1929.

People always arrived at LaGrave Field early because no reserve seats existed. Some patrons rented cushions for ten cents. During the week, the management let kids in free to the west stadium if the game was not a big one and seats remained. But there were probably no free seats when Babe Ruth and Lou Gehrig played exhibition games at LaGrave Field during the 1920s.[13]

In the 1930s, LaGrave Field held the distinction of being the only baseball park in the Texas League circuit to provide a separate clubhouse for the visiting team. When night baseball began in the Texas League, promoters of LaGrave installed a modern lighting plant. It cost $23,000 in the Depression year of 1930, but Fort Worthians supported their baseball team enough to permit the owners to afford it. To get full use out of the expensively lit field, owners allowed local high schools to play football games there during the fall season.[14]

Soon after World War II, the Fort Worth Cats became a member of the Dodger major league organization and served as a "Double-A" farm team. Prior to that the Cats operated as an independent team and sometimes sold their players' contracts to the big leagues.

Rogers Hornsby, a local North Side boy, managed the Cats during the 1945-1946 seasons. Hornsby joined the majors in 1915 and played until 1937, primarily as a second baseman for the St. Louis Cardinals. In his twenty-three years in the big leagues,

*Modern, well-lighted LaGrave Field was the home of the Fort
Worth Cats for five decades (courtesy A. M. Pate, Jr., and
Texas Refinery Corporation).*

Hornsby participated in two world series, and was considered by
some to be baseball's greatest right-handed hitter. His career bat-
ting average of .358 secured him a place on most people's all-time
great team, and he was certainly the greatest baseball player ever
to come out of Fort Worth.

Other Cats managers after the war included Ray Hayworth, Les
Burge, and Bobby Bragan. Bragan served as a player-manager of
the Cats from 1948 to 1952 and won two Texas League championships during those five seasons. On the field he played catcher.

Bragan, who came immediately from the Brooklyn Dodgers to
Fort Worth in June 1948, recalls several incidents that happened
during his tenure with the Cats. In 1949, LaGrave Field burned
down. The bleachers caught fire about 11:30 P.M., after the game
ended, and were soon a total loss. "We never determined what
caused it," Bragan said.[15]

The Cats played the next afternoon with 3,000 spectators sitting on the grass and on temporary wooden bleachers erected that morning. The steel girders left from the original bleachers remained hot to the touch at game time. President of the club, John L. Reeves, rebuilt the park, completely out of steel with new bleachers seating 12,000, by the 1950 season.[16]

One of Bragan's players during his years with the Cats was a young man from Caracas, Venezuela, named Chico Carrasquel who played ball in the States while his wife remained in Venezuela. On a special Chico Carrasquel night at the park, club president John Reeves arranged secretly to bring Carrasquel's wife to the game. While officials honored the young shortstop at home plate with gifts of western boots, hat, and other paraphernalia, the club owner brought out his wife, who had never been to this country before. "There were a lot of teary eyes that night," Bragan remembered.[17]

Stories like these demonstrate the close relationship that existed between the team and its hometown fans, with the team seeming more like a family than an investment or a corporate entity. Managers might change, but the family spirit remained. Following Bragan as manager of the Cats were Max Macon, Gene Handley, Al Vincent, and Lou Klein.[18]

As baseball became "Big Business" in the 1950s, the local relationships also changed. When the Dodgers, the Cats major league counterpart, moved from Brooklyn to Los Angeles in 1958, they swapped ownership of LaGrave Field to the Chicago Cubs. In 1965, the Cubs moved the team to Turnpike Stadium to create the Dallas-Fort Worth Spurs. The Spurs later became the Texas Rangers when the Washington Senators moved to Texas. It was the end of an era.

The Fort Worth Cats had ceased to exist as a club in 1965, and fans saw no more Texas League baseball played on the North Side at LaGrave Field. The League team had called Fort Worth home for more than seventy-five years. In 1974, A. M. Pate, Jr., of the Texas Refinery Corporation, purchased the eighteen acres of LaGrave Field to expand his company's facilities. And so LaGrave Field passed into North Side history. Some had called it "the best ball park in the minor leagues."[19]

The record of the Fort Worth Cats speaks for itself. During their seventy-five years in the Texas League, the Cats won fourteen pennants — 1895, 1905, 1920-1925, 1930, 1937, 1939, 1948-1949, and 1958. Some Cats players who made names for themselves in the big leagues while the club was part of the Dodgers organization include: Cal Abrams, Sparky Anderson, Wayne Belardi, Chico Carrasquel, Gene Cimoli, Carl Erskine, Elroy Pace, Dee Fondy, Don Hoak, Billy Hunter, Bob Milliken, Ray Moore, Danny Ozark, Carl Spooner, Preston Ward, and Dick Williams. Anderson and Williams, after their playing days, became highly successful major league managers — Williams with the San Diego Padres and Anderson with the Detroit Tigers.

Billy Hunter is a special case in the story of local baseball. He came "home" to manage the present-day Texas Rangers during two seasons — from July 1, 1977, through the 1978 campaign. Under his management the team won ninety-four games, but like so many Rangers managers, Hunter did not stay around long enough to see the team become successful.

Although football is not as strongly associated with the North Side, several local boys achieved national pigskin fame. Even World War I raging in their European homelands did not keep North Side families from enjoying high school football. Most could at least forget the ominous events in the old country for a while on Friday nights as they cheered the North Side High School Steers on to two state championships in 1915 and 1916.

Robert L. "Chief" Myers coached the team. Myers had been living in Chicago when he heard that North Side needed an English teacher who could also coach athletics. He had earned a degree from Centre College at Danville, Kentucky, and was qualified to teach, but the closest he had come to coaching had been watching lectures and demonstrations by the football coach at a Chicago university. Myers had not even been a successful football player despite his love for the game.[20] Apparently, the Fort Worth Board of Education considered Myers's English teaching credentials more important than any coaching or playing experience.

North Side High School had only been playing football three years when Myers arrived in 1912. The first team he coached made an improvement over previous years but remained only average. The next three years, the team set records. In 1913, they lost only one game during season play; the next year they lost only the state championship game in Austin. Finally came the two seasons — 1915 and 1916 — when the team won the state title.[21]

Those who knew Coach Myers back in Danville, Kentucky, heard about his success as a coach in Texas. Centre College persuaded him to leave North Side to coach the Danville Colonels. Within three years, a dozen of his North Side championship players had followed him to Danville, encouraged in their decision by scholarships. In 1919, 1920, and 1921, the "Praying Colonels" —so-called because of a ritual pre-game team prayer — made football history and gained national attention as they won game after game.[22]

Harvard had won twenty-five consecutive games in the 1921 season before they met Centre College. When former North Sider "Bo" McMillin ran for a thirty-two-yard touchdown, the Colonels won 6-0. Sportscasters called the win "the biggest surprise in football history."[23] In five years Centre won thirty-eight games, lost four, and scored 1,757 points to 121 for their opponents.[24] During those years, North Siders were always anxious to receive their *Fort Worth Star-Telegram* to see how their boys up in Kentucky had fared.

In later years, another North Side boy made a name for himself in football. Yale Lary, who grew up on Lincoln Avenue, graduated from North Side High School in 1948 as its star football player. Most Southwest Conference teams tried to recruit him; he chose Texas A & M University. During his senior year he was chosen most valuable player. He later enjoyed a brilliant eleven-year career with the Detroit Lions, playing on three championship teams in 1952, 1953, and 1957.[25] Lary was named All-Pro four times and played in the Pro Bowl nine times. In 1979, he was inducted into the Pro Football Hall of Fame in Canton, Ohio.[26]

Numerous North Siders made a name for themselves in other sports. North Side High School track star Elmer Helbing, son of former North Side physician Dr. H. V. Helbing, set several records and once tied a world mark in the 220-yard race. As a high school senior in 1933, Helbing traveled to Chicago to compete with the holder of the 220 record; he placed second. The first-place winner who went on to gain fame in the 1936 Olympics in Berlin was Jesse Owens. Helbing received a scholarship to Louisiana State University but stayed only a short time before coming back to attend Texas Christian University. He set a 100-yard record for the TCU Horned Frogs while there.[27]

All in all, whether baseball, football, or track, North Fort Worth has enjoyed its share of sports greats.

10
Demographics
Favor Hispanics

From the earliest days, a small settlement of shacks along the Trinity River bottoms east of Harding Street was home for families of African-American descent. Generally, they worked for families or businesses "up on the bluff" in Fort Worth.[1] By the 1920s and 1930s a black settlement stretched from Twenty-eighth Street out Angle Avenue directly north of Rosen Heights, starting at about the 2500 block of Clinton Avenue. A school for black children was also located on Clinton.

But even though the earliest immigrants were from central and eastern Europe, and though African-Americans have lived on the North Side for many years, the community today is dominated by Hispanics and their culture.

Spanish is spoken frequently, and Hispanic immigrants continue to move into the older neighborhoods. Historically, Hispanic immigration developed in three fairly distinct phases. The first lasted for over a century as Mexican citizens trickled into Texas, Arizona, and California with most newcomers remaining fairly close to the border. In the early 1900s, only a few brave souls migrated north to Fort Worth to settle on the North Side along with the immigrants from central and eastern Europe. The revolution in Mexico which began in 1910, sparked part of this early migration, which lasted until just before World War I.

Triggered by the demand for labor in World War I and the period of prosperity after the war, the second phase (1918-1930s) brought additional workers from Mexico to the packing plants on the North Side. Then during the Great Depression, immigration slowed.

A third, much larger phase of Mexican immigration to the North Side, came with the demand during World War II for labor when no quotas were placed on Mexican immigration to the United States. Often U.S. officials interpreted restrictions on disease, illiteracy, and likelihood of being a welfare recipient leniently if they believed that U.S. agriculture or industry needed more laborers.[2]

One of the best known Mexican immigrants of the early phase is Joe T. Garcia. Garcia and the young lady who later became his wife, Jesus, both grew up in the small Mexican town of Yrecuro, but they did not meet until their families settled on the North Side. Since there were few Mexican immigrants in North Fort Worth in those days, the few families naturally banded together. Joe, sixteen when he arrived in 1914, was raised by an uncle, John S. Garcia, who became a meat dealer and grocer.[3]

As soon as Garcia arrived in the area, he went to work for Armour and Company where he remained for about twenty years. Even then he planned and dreamed of something better. While working for Armour, he resold meat to Leonard Brothers and other grocery stores. In this way he learned how to run a business. In 1919, he and his uncle started a grocery store at 2140 North Commerce. As a sideline, Joe sold barbecue and Mexican food in the store.

His wife, Jesus, known as "Mama Sus," cooked lunches to sell. She had been cooking since the age of seven when her mother died and she became the family cook for her father and brothers. "Mama Sus" was a good cook and attracted a lot of people from Armour and Swift to the Garcia grocery store to eat during their lunch hour. Joe would even take orders at work, rush to the store to pick them up, and then deliver them back to the plant—all on his own lunchtime.[4]

Soon, the Garcias began making more money selling the lunches than they were earning from the grocery store. This prompted Joe to purchase the white frame house at 2201 North Commerce. It was to become famous as "Joe's Place" and later better known as "Joe T. Garcia's." The little house had formerly been a residence,

then a Greek bar. The bar had gone out of business, and city officials condemned the building before Garcia bought it and renovated it. He began his new venture on July 4, 1935.

The Garcia family lived in a white house with pink trim on
Twenty-second Street, just out the back door from the restaurant.
Garcia, a friendly and talkative person, attracted people to his
restaurant. He remembered everyone's name and came out and
visited with his customers as though they were guests in his own
home. He always asked how their families were doing. "Papa loved
friends better than money. That's why his cafe was so well
known," his daughter, Mary Garcia, once explained.[5]

Soon, important people from all over Fort Worth began coming
to his restaurant. Amon G. Carter, publisher of the *Fort Worth
Star-Telegram,* liked to entertain out-of-town guests there. News
stories mentioning the restaurant certainly helped attract new
customers. Garcia had autographed pictures of three presidents of
Mexico and three Texas governors among his mementos. Also
helpful in attracting customers was son-in-law Paul Lancarte who
studied business at Texas Christian University and invited his fellow students and their families to the restaurant.[6]

Joe's Place had no menu in those days; everyone ordered the
family dinner. If a customer wanted a refill, he just came to the
kitchen and got it. In fact, going through the kitchen to the dining room was a tradition until about 1980, when remodeling and
health department regulations mandated a change.

Although family members are not sure of the exact date, about
1948 or 1949, the name of the restaurant was changed from "Joe's
Place" to "Joe T. Garcia's." When Garcia passed away in 1953,
"Mama Sus" took over and ran the restaurant with the help of her
daughter Hope and son-in-law Lancarte. "Mama Sus" lived to age
ninety and cooked for the restaurant for many of those years.

Joe T. Garcia's valued its customers' honesty. Up until 1970, the
restaurant did not even give checks with the meal. At the cash
register the customer simply told what he had eaten and paid for
it. The family added more variety to the menu about that time
and also expanded the premises, building a patio. They have continued to expand over the years until the restaurant covers nearly
half of the 2200 block of North Commerce.[7]

Another North Side Hispanic whose roots go back to the earliest migration is Pris Dominguez, an artist whose work has been displayed all over Fort Worth. In the 1970s, he completed major art work for the Texas Rangers baseball club. He also served as president for one term and a ten-year board member for the Fort Worth Hispanic Chamber of Commerce.[8]

According to Dominguez's sister Celia, their parents came to Fort Worth as young children. Her grandparents later returned to Mexico, but her father, Jose Jesus Dominguez, having married in 1918, stayed. He ran a small grocery store, so the family of six children had plenty to eat during the Depression.[9]

However, when Jose Dominguez lost money during the Depression by giving credit to people who could not pay, he turned the grocery store over to his wife and began working at one of the packing houses. In his spare time, he also sold insurance for Woodmen of the World and played a coronet and clarinet with a band at the Bohemian Club on Jacksboro Highway. "For a time there Dad had four jobs," Celia said.[10]

Her brother Pris, born in 1926, served in the Navy in World War II. After he returned to Fort Worth, he studied art at Texas Christian University, and in 1951 became one of the first North Side Hispanics to graduate from TCU. An artist-designer, Dominguez worked from 1951 to 1963 as art director for several agencies and as a package designer and staff artist for a packaging corporation. During the next ten years, he was consulting art director for Jerre R. Todd and Associates. He had his own art studio from 1973 until his death in November 1990. Well known for his portraits of sports greats, Dominguez completed ninety-nine black-and-white drawings for the TCU Sports Hall of Fame in Daniel Meyer Coliseum. He designed sporting event programs for TCU, the Texas Rangers, and the Dallas Cowboys.[11]

J. Pete Zepeda is another success story among early Hispanic families on the North Side. His mother was descended from a Spanish family that had settled in Texas nearly two hundred years earlier. His father came from Monclova, Coahuilla, in northern Mexico. Zepeda himself was born in Nacogdoches but the family came to Fort Worth in 1915 in a covered wagon, taking two weeks to travel from Nacogdoches. In Fort Worth, the elder

Zepeda worked for a paving construction company that built Camp Bowie Boulevard out of Thurber brick. Pete attended the old M. G. Ellis School and then J. P. Elder when it was new in 1927. He studied printing at the vocational high school, attended North Side High School, and completed over two years of classes at Texas Wesleyan during the Depression.

After working as a printer and in the export department of Texas Refinery, Zepeda worked at General Dynamics until his retirement in 1984. In addition, he and his wife ran a tax, real estate, and insurance business for Hispanics, often helping newly arrived immigrants with translations of their legal documents. His wife often interpreted for the newcomers in court. Zepeda became the first Hispanic on the Tarrant County Junior College District Board when he was appointed to replace Loyd Cox in February 1983. He has been re-elected twice.

Zepeda explained that when he first tried to purchase a house west of North Main in the 1940s, he could not because of discrimination against Hispanics. The earliest Hispanic immigrants lived in a small barrio which started at Twenty-third Street and stretched to North Side Drive, thus living alongside immigrants from central and eastern Europe. The European immigrants began to move to Rosen Heights where they could easily buy houses, but the Hispanics faced hostility if they even tried to cross Main Street to attend free movies at Marine Park.

A few aggressive young men tested the situation occasionally by sauntering west of Main, but most parents urged their children to avoid conflicts and stay close to home. Angry gangs on either side often threw bottles and rocks at each other, sometimes knocking out teeth or causing more serious injuries.[12]

Still, many Mexicans wanted to move across Main Street where the streets were paved and houses sold for $3,000 to $7,000. On the east side of the dividing street, shacks sold for between $100 and $500 and there were no paved streets.[13] Anglo homeowners formed the Fostepco Heights and Diamond Hill civic leagues to prevent Hispanics from moving into their neighborhoods, and real estate agents worked with the homeowners to find housing elsewhere for the Hispanics.[14] But World War II marked the beginning of a period of expansion of Hispanic neighborhoods, and in the economic prosperity of the late 1940s and early 1950s, the Hispanic demand for housing west of North Main and in Diamond Hill became too great. Those areas gradually opened to Hispanic buyers and renters. Zepeda, who had moved to the Polytechnic area, returned to the North Side.[15]

~

The Beltram family came to Fort Worth during the second period of migration (1918 to 1930s). Hector, oldest of seven children, explained that his father Jesus (Jessie) met his mother Laura Carrera, a schoolteacher, in Milano, the county seat of Rockdale County, where Jessie worked as a coal miner. The family moved to Bridgeport around 1926 when Hector was five. His father worked in coal mines there until they closed. After farming a year, Jessie brought his family to the Mexican community on the North Side in the early 1930s. The family of nine lived in a company house belonging to the Fort Worth Cotton Oil Mill on Decatur Avenue until the 1940s. Hector Beltram remembered that families in the eight or nine company houses were a mixed lot: a couple of Anglo families, three or four Hispanic families, and the rest black.

Hector, who graduated from Diamond Hill High School in 1940, joined the military during World War II. When he returned to Fort Worth in December 1945, his parents had moved to Rosen Heights.[16]

Hector Beltram's family presents a good example of the three-generation pattern that occurred in most of the Hispanic families that arrived in either the first or second migration into the North Side. Jessie and Laura Beltram and their seven children worked extremely hard, living in the small company house until their children were nearly grown. Jessie used to tell Hector: "Son, I worked like a dog for years and years and haven't accomplished anything. I hope you accomplish something."[17]

Hector did. He retired from the Air Force and Department of Defense after thirty-one years, set up a small business, and moved to the North Side area west of Main Street. His children, the third generation, moved out of the North Side and scattered all over the city as they completed educations and pursued careers. His oldest son, Hector Beltram, Jr., became a vice-principal at

The Garcia family (top) stands ready to welcome their first customers on opening day, July 4, 1935. They are (left to right) Mary, Josephine, Hope, Pauline, and Joe T. Garcia (courtesy Joe T. Garcia's Restaurant). Below, board members of the Fort Worth Hispanic Chamber of Commerce in the early 1980s when the organization began. Standing left to right are Bob McKinley, executive director, J. Pete Zepeda, Hector Gutierrez, Charles Tegethoff, Hector Beltram, and John McMillan. Sitting are Albert Cano, Pris Dominguez, and Abel Sanchez (courtesy the Fort Worth Hispanic Chamber of Commerce).

Southwest High School. His daughter Linda Ann taught at W. C. Stripling Middle School, and his youngest son Robert became a commander in the Navy, serving as a chaplain at a naval base in New Orleans.

Although Jessie died in the 1970s, Laura Beltram lived to be ninety-four and saw the educational and economic successes of her grandchildren.[18]

Hispanic families often kept close relationships with extended-family members — aunts, uncles, grandparents, cousins, in-laws, and even godparents.[19] The 350 persons who attended an Ayala family reunion in 1992 are testimony to this.[20] Eutimio and Maria Ortiz Ayala migrated to the United States in 1917 after their marriage in Mexico. Eutimio worked for a car company in Detroit for a while and then moved to Ohio and Indiana, where he worked in sugar-beet fields during the season. The family moved to Fort Worth about 1934, living east of North Main Street in the barrio. Ayala got a job at Swift and Company to support his family of fourteen children. One of these children, Michael, born in Blufton, Indiana in 1927, remembered some of his sisters earning $24 per month working at St. Joseph's Hospital. In 1938 or 1939, the family bought a reasonably priced home on two lots at 1212 North Grove.[21]

Michael Ayala and his extended family provide an additional example of how second- and third-generation Hispanics prospered after the hard work of their parents. About ten years after being discharged from the Merchant Marine, Michael found a job with the U.S. Postal Service in 1957 and worked thirty-five years until his retirement in 1992. He worked in Ridglea before being transferred to the North Side branch in 1959.

Michael's children are all graduates of Texas Christian University. His son Carlos served as a principal at Rosemont Middle School and later as an assistant administrator in the Fort Worth Public School administration building. His daughter Dolores Ayala Rios is an elementary teacher, and daughter Teresa works for American Airlines in the Spanish international department.

His siblings have prospered as well. One brother, Louis, was a barber on North Main for over forty-five years. Another brother began a thriving Mexican restaurant in Granbury.

Michael saw a "certain amount of prejudice" as he grew up on the North Side; however, he said that "it worked both ways" as troublesome Hispanics from east of North Main would go over to the other side to pick a fight, and Anglo youngsters from west of Main would "come over here." He believed that once each side respected the other, and the Anglos "saw we were hardworking, we didn't have any trouble with discrimination. . . . I never had any real problems." Ayala said, however, in his post office job he saw a little initial hesitancy and distrust. "I just kept being friendly. Some of those people later became my best friends."[22]

Michael Ayala's wife, Esperanza Padilla, whom he met at San Jose Catholic School, has worked at All Saints Catholic Church since 1961. The histories of All Saints and San Jose Catholic churches parallel and help explain the growth of the Hispanic population on the North Side.

Beginning in the spring of 1902, all the area north of the Trinity River was the new All Saints Parish. Families worshipping at All Saints Catholic Church were usually meat-packing personnel transferred from Chicago or immigrant families from Europe.

The Iglesia de San Jose opened as a chapel early in 1909 to care for the spiritual needs of Mexican immigrants. The wooden chapel was in the All Saints Parish, a few blocks from the original church. San Jose moved to North Commerce and East Fourteenth streets in 1919, and in 1930 a brick building replaced the frame structure.[23] The parish operated a parochial school in which English was spoken and written. In addition, the church provided a free clinic and a number of social and educational opportunities.[24]

On February 11, 1955, San Jose and All Saints merged. The church entrusted the entire parish to the Claretian fathers who had been administering San Jose Mission. They made the San Jose building into a center for youth, but later it became a Catholic men's clubhouse.[25]

The merger in 1955 created a bilingual, bicultural parish. By 1955, Mexicans were moving west of North Main Street and settling around All Saints Church. When the merger occurred, there were 350 families in each parish. Membership kept increasing and reached 1,500 families after two decades. At the start of the 1990s, All Saints Catholic Church membership was ninety-eight percent Hispanic.[26] The Mexican community of the All Saints Parish celebrates *el Cinco de Mayo* and *el Diez y Seis de Septiembre*, both Mexican fiestas, across Twentieth Street from the church at Marine Park.[27]

The Catholics were not the only religious group active in the Hispanic community in the early years. The Methodists purchased a former two-story saloon and gambling place in the 1920s at 2139 North Commerce (across from Joe T. Garcia's later grocery site) and tore it down to construct a church.[28] As early as 1915, the Methodists also operated a Wesley Community Center with a kindergarten. The community center housed a library of English-language books, a reading room, a Saturday morning free clinic, and other social activities. Cooking, sewing, and piano lessons were offered in the 1930s.[29]

A Hispanic Baptist Church was located at 500 East Central a bit later. These three denominations — Catholic, Methodist, and Baptist — were the only ones in the Hispanic community for quite some time.[30]

The third and much larger migration of Hispanics from Mexico came after the 1950s, bringing lower income workers at a time when meat-packing and railroad jobs began to decline. Because these later arrivals were first-generation immigrants, they have not resided in the North Side long enough to prosper like the second and third generations of the Garcia, Dominguez, Zepeda, Beltram, or Ayala families. While today new arrivals can live anywhere in the North Side — and do — they face difficulties in finding employment that earlier immigrants found readily available. They often lack the education necessary to secure well-paid jobs. These first-generation immigrants tend to marry young and have large families. Consequently, unemployment, welfare, crime, and housing decay have become facts of life in much of the near North Side as well as Diamond Hill, Rosen Heights and other communities.

Carlos Puente, who came to Fort Worth from Galveston in

1972 with his wife Maria Esther, provides an exception to the pattern but does give an example of the third and latest migration of Hispanics. The Puentes lived in the south part of Fort Worth for a year before moving to the North Side. Puente earned a Masters degree in urban affairs from the University of Texas at Arlington in 1973, after having received an undergraduate degree in political science two years earlier from the University of North Texas. He put his political knowledge to use when he became the first Hispanic to serve on the board of the Fort Worth Independent School District from 1978 to 1984. In 1991, he won an election to represent the North Side on the Fort Worth City Council, replacing Louis Zapata who had been the first Hispanic to serve on the city council after single member districts came into being. Puente has been active in the North Side Neighborhood Association as well.[31]

The accomplishments of both Louis Zapata and Carlos Puente suggest that Hispanics are getting politically organized and waging successful campaigns since the advent of single-member districts. However, some of the progress made by Hispanics has been due to Rufino Mendoza, Sr., who was the main spokesman for the Hispanic community in a school desegregation judgment in 1981. Mendoza, chairman and a founding member of the Fort Worth Mexican-American Educational Advisory Committee, pointed out that when he filed his judgment based on a prior 1971 lawsuit, only two Hispanic administrators worked in the Fort Worth ISD. By the early 1990s there were sixty. He also protested at-large places on the Fort Worth School Board, claiming that minorities did not have an equal chance to win these seats. Mendoza also lobbied the Fort Worth Police Department in 1986 to promote more Hispanic-surnamed officers.[32]

Some of the more successful North Side Hispanics do not credit politics or political representation for a better life. They cite education and better jobs as the sources of a rise in their standard of living. "It helps to own your own business. Then you know that you aren't going to be laid off," explained Bennie Cordona, who once worked seven days a week delivering pastries from his father's bakery. Cordona eventually took over the bakery and ran the business until his retirement.

Further evidence of profitable ethnic organization is the Fort Worth Hispanic Chamber of Commerce, which has offices in the former Vinnedge Building at 2100 North Main Street. The chamber began in 1973 with a small group of about thirty minority business leaders, first calling themselves the Fort Worth Mexican-American Chamber of Commerce. In 1974, it became the fourth Mexican-American chamber to be established in the state of Texas.[33]

In 1983, the members of the organization changed the name to Fort Worth Hispanic Chamber of Commerce. The primary focus of the chamber is economic development for the community, particularly for small businesses because they create most of the jobs. The chamber hosts seminars, gives marketing assistance, and provides networking opportunities for Hispanic business owners. Approximately two-thirds of the three hundred members are Hispanic-owned businesses. Other chamber members include corporations which are interested in marketing their products to Hispanics. In Fort Worth, the Hispanic market is growing five times faster than the general market.[34]

A secondary focus of the Hispanic Chamber is an educational program aimed at keeping Hispanic youth in school. In four middle schools with over a thirty-five percent Hispanic enrollment, the Hispanic Chamber of Commerce grants $600 college scholarships to eighth-graders with the stipulation that they only receive the money, plus interest, when they graduate from high school and enroll in college.[35]

In less than half a century the demographic composition of the North Side has changed considerably. From the earlier, booming livestock market with its stockyards and numerous meat-packing facilities that fostered the name "Cowtown," the business section along North Main Street in the 1990s is comprised of small establishments catering mostly to the Hispanic market. Only on Exchange Avenue and North Main streets, adjacent to the stockyards, can one find the western businesses that seek the dollars of the tourist trade.

11
That
North Side Spirit
Lingers

While some proper Fort Worthians from south of the Trinity may have looked down their noses at the sights and sounds — not to mention the smells — of the North Side, they all shared something in common. Pioneer Texans from both sides of the river — rich and poor, Anglo, black and immigrant — are laid to rest north of the bluff. In an unusual blend of the history and heritage, the two oldest local cemeteries hold the remains of Fort Worth's founding fathers.

Pioneer's Rest Cemetery, in the 600 block of Samuels Avenue, originated in 1850 as the site where the two young children of Major Ripley Arnold were buried. Sophie and Willis (or Willie) Arnold died of unknown causes while their father commanded the troops who established Fort Worth. Dr. Adolphus Gouhenant, a local physician of French background, donated some of his own land for the graves.

Arnold was killed in 1853 in a duel at Fort Graham, where he was then stationed. Friends buried the officer at Fort Graham, but the following year community leaders in Fort Worth arranged to have his body brought to Tarrant County to be interred beside his two children. A monument stands over his grave and two small tombstones identify those of his children. They are located in the extreme southwestern portion of the expanded cemetery.[1]

A group of interested citizens formed the Pioneer's Rest Cemetery Association in 1870. The following year Baldwin L.

Samuels donated three more acres. General Edward H. Tarrant, for whom the county is named, is also buried at Pioneer's Rest Cemetery. Although he died in 1858 in Parker County, his family moved his body to Ellis County the next year. Seventy years after his death, a movement began in Fort Worth to rebury the general in the county named for him. Fort Worth citizens reinterred his body in 1928 with full military honors.[2]

John Peter Smith donated a plot of twenty acres in 1879 to Fort Worth, the first land for what later became Oakwood Cemetery at 800 Grand Avenue. The section for blacks was called Trinity Cemetery, the part for whites, New City Cemetery (Old City Cemetery being Pioneer's Rest), and in 1880, a part was partitioned off for Catholics and called Calvary. The state of Texas issued a charter to the Oakwood Cemetery Association in 1909; a five-member board, appointed by the city of Fort Worth, still administers the 100-plus acre cemetery.[3]

Some called the cemetery "Cowtown's Boot Hill."[4] Bricklayers, bartenders, and even gunslingers Luke Short and Timothy "Longhair Jim" Courtright lie close together on the tree-shaded hill of Oakwood near the banks of the west fork of the Trinity. The tallest monument in Oakwood is a spire erected by William "Gooseneck Bill" McDonald, a wealthy black Fort Worth businessman. He purchased the monument to honor his son. Later two of his wives were laid to rest under large markers. Surprisingly, McDonald provided no additional marker to be placed on his own grave.[5] Other structures at Oakwood include a statue of a Confederate soldier standing guard over a section called "Soldier's Row," and a chapel at the north gate called the "Westminster Abbey of Fort Worth."[6]

Those from the north and the south also share a common bond of history and economics in North Fort Worth that is preserved in large part by the North Fort Worth Historical Society (NFWHS). Upset because he could do nothing to save the historic city hall of Niles City on Decatur Avenue from being torn down, the late Charlie McCafferty, native North Sider, proposed creating the

NFWHS in 1975. Officially chartered in the 1976 bicentennial year, the society has been able to preserve many historic sites and buildings. Charlie's wife, Sue McCafferty, has served as president of the society for a decade and a half and has shaped it into a strong and influential organization.

Today, the North Fort Worth Historical Society fosters the continued mingling of spirits old and new by sponsoring a Fourth of July picnic in Oakwood Cemetery. Modern North Fort Worth folks and others from across the city mingle with the spirits of the city's oldest and greatest leaders each summer, when the North Fort Worth Historical Society hosts an old-fashioned patriotic picnic under the shade of the spreading oak trees of the graveyard. After the food has disappeared, a few members of the historical society dress up and impersonate Luke Short, John Peter Smith, Burk Burnett, and other North Siders of the past, entertaining the members and guests with accounts of "their" lives. At dusk, members move to the side of the hill facing the Trinity River and downtown Fort Worth to watch the traditional forty-five minute fireworks display.[7] With dusk caretakers throw open the iron cemetery gates so that all residents of the neighborhoods around Oakwood can fill the hillside for an excellent view of the stupendous fireworks show.

The North Fort Worth Historical Society preserves the livestock heritage that created the western atmosphere dominating Exchange Avenue and the entire Stockyards National Historic District. Texas historical markers dot the landscape throughout the area. In its Stockyards Collection and Museum, a free exhibit area in the Livestock Exchange Building, NFWHS preserves important records and artifacts that highlight the livestock image, not only of the North Side but of all of Fort Worth. With the continuing efforts to preserve the historic buildings and the livestock legacy of Fort Worth, NFWHS has been a major factor in nourishing interest in the North Side.

The North Side has long attracted visitors passing though Fort Worth, starting with the days when drovers bedded down their cattle as they trailed them northward. Even though people had been coming to the stockyards for years, it was not until they practically stopped coming after the livestock market declined that local citizens realized they needed to do something to get tourists back. As early as 1955, businessmen on the North Side began to notice that their section of town was not growing and prospering like other areas of the city. They needed better street lighting, medical facilities for their citizens, more industries, and more off-street parking. They believed that an organization to supplement the Fort Worth Chamber of Commerce might achieve these goals. In October 1955, these entrepreneurs created the North Side Business Association (later renamed North Fort Worth Business Association). R. G. McElyea was the first president. To attract visitors, McElyea leased out the North Side Coliseum for boxing on Monday nights, country-western singing on Saturday nights, and numerous other activities in between.[8]

The next year the NFWBA decided to sponsor a "go western" event calling Saturday, April 28, "Pioneer Day," and dedicating it "to the recapture of a bit of the spirit of the Old West and North Fort Worth's place in the metropolitan area's business picture."[9] The day brought the largest crowd to Exchange Avenue since stock show days, especially the sundown ceremony of turning on the twenty-two new vapor-mercury streetlights along Exchange Avenue. Five more new lights burned on North Commerce by the coliseum.[10]

The association made "Pioneer Days" an annual event and even urged businesses along Exchange Avenue and the nearby blocks on North Main Street to put wooden fronts on their buildings and awnings over the sidewalks to enhance the western image. Oak and redwood posts supported rustic wooden awnings. During the third annual Pioneer Days in 1958, businessmen staged an official opening of "Cowtown, U.S.A" to show off the renovated four-block area around North Main and Exchange.[11]

The association even convinced the city of Fort Worth to include $1,200,000 for a western village on a bond election November 18, 1958. Funds would be for a tourist hotel, an animal exhibit, Indian and western villages, parking, a small lake, and a museum; voters, however, turned down the proposal.[12]

By 1971, Fort Worth civic leaders saw that the North Side should be redeveloped to help the city's economy. Fort Worth was falling behind Dallas in convention bookings, and city fathers saw the North Side as a potential tourist attraction even though it had become an area of unemployment and decay after Armour and Swift shut their doors.[13] The City Council appointed a sixteen-member Stockyards Area Restoration Committee (SARC) in April 1972 to supervise both public and private redevelopment. A grandson of Dave Shannon, Jack, chaired the committee.[14]

On recommendation of the committee, the city of Fort Worth applied for federal funds from the Economic Development Administration and made the Stockyards Restoration Project an official bicentennial project. Included in the redevelopment were the restoration of a brick surface to Exchange Avenue, sidewalk reconstruction, decorative lighting on Exchange Avenue, and street furniture and landscaping. Marine Creek was landscaped from Exchange Avenue to Twenty-third Street.[15]

Canal-Randolph, the real estate development corporation that owned United Stockyards, parent company of the Fort Worth Stockyards, spent $750,000 in 1978 to renovate the Livestock Exchange Building with plans to lease 29,000 square feet for office space. With the opening in April 1981 of Billy Bob's Texas, billed as the largest honky-tonk in the world, visitors began to return to the stockyards area. The site for Billy Bob's, a building constructed in 1936 to house additional exhibits for the stock show, stretches three acres in size.[16]

Finding investors with enough private money to develop shops, restaurants, and the like under one ownership proved to be a problem in the 1980s. Even Billy Bob Barnett, owner of the club bearing his name, had financial problems and had to close the club for a few months. As the 1990s began, two major local investors managed to put together plans to develop the area with private funds. Holt Hickman and his associates took out a five-year lease on the Exchange Building and twenty acres around it. Calling his project "Stockyards Station," Hickman built a Spanish-style tourist information center across from the Livestock Exchange, managed the leasing of the property, and planned amusement-park-type attractions on the land between Marine Creek and Exchange Avenue. He hired Burt Shield to run the weekly livestock auctions and still kept an actual livestock market in operation until December 1992 when the market closed.

William Davis, the second major investor, concentrated on his Fort Worth and Western Railroad and on bringing a steam-driven train to the stockyards. This train, a strong tourist attraction, will eventually move visitors from the stockyards area to downtown Fort Worth, the museum district, Forest Park, and even Dallas, Cleburne, and Granbury. Davis used the name Tarantula Railroad, recalling an article in an 1873 Fort Worth newspaper in which editor Buckley B. Paddock drew a map showing Fort Worth as the railroad center of North Texas.[17] Paddock was being optimistic; when he drew his map Fort Worth did not have even one railroad. A Dallas newspaperman ridiculed Paddock's map and his optimism, saying the crude sketch looked like a "tarantula." Paddock and Fort Worthians enjoyed the last laugh, however: by the turn of the century Cowtown did indeed welcome at least ten railroad lines.

Davis worked closely with Ed McLaughlin, a Fort Worth native who has built railroad excursion trains in East Texas, Colorado, and various other parts of the world. With track engineer Ted Brown, Davis and McLaughlin became modern-day Paddocks, capitalizing on Fort Worth's image as "Cowtown" to attract visitors. Davis used some of the old tracks still available and the concrete shed which receives the train before it reaches the turntable on the north side of Exchange Avenue once covered the stockyards sheep pens in the 1940s.

Rodeo has also been reborn in the area. For a decade beginning in the 1970s, Steve Murrin operated a rodeo in the North Side Coliseum, or Cowtown Coliseum, as it is now called. The arena is owned by the city of Fort Worth, purchased from the Fort Worth Stockyards Company in 1936. Murrin withdrew when the city obtained a federal grant and renovated the coliseum, completing the task in 1986. The city then created an organization called Friends of the North Side Coliseum to provide rodeo activities again each Saturday night of an extended summer season. Murrin has since once again become the moving spirit behind the rodeo.

Murrin and his colleague, Joe Dulle, have been two of the most loyal entrepreneurs in the stockyards area for over twenty years. Between them, they own many of the buildings and businesses on West Exchange Avenue and the first block of East Exchange.

The sign near the intersection of North Main and Exchange at the entrance to the refurbished stockyards is a familiar sight to local visitors and a welcome to out-of-town tourists (North Fort Worth Historical Society).

They have been leaders in bringing tourism and business back to the area.

A company called Cowtown Corrals, owned by Keith Kothmann and Jerome Stock, purchased three-and-a-half acres at 500 Northeast Twenty-third Street, on the south edge of the stockyards, in mid-summer 1992. The owners take horseback riders from the stockyards area to the northern edge of downtown along trails in the Trinity River basin. The trails are located on 250 acres leased from the U.S. Army Corps of Engineers. Kothmann and Stock turned a former pipe-manufacturing plant into a combination stables and party barn where they host camp fires, rodeos, and similar western entertainment in addition to the trail rides.[18]

Several annual activities celebrate Fort Worth's western heritage: A Cowtown Marathon in February, Chisholm Trail Roundup in mid-June, Pioneer Days in September, and Christmastime in the Stockyards. Rodeos and riding events in the Cowtown Coliseum keep the area an exhibition of the Old West in action for the hordes of tourists and homefolks who continue to wander Exchange Avenue. On any given day, tourists signing the guest register at the historical society's museum may hail from Germany, Great Britain, Georgia, Canada, California, Czechoslovakia, or just about anywhere.

The North Side is the reason Fort Worth is Cowtown. It is "the tail that wagged the dog," Dave Shannon once said. His daughter, Juanita McCain, explained that Shannon apparently meant that before a political candidate could carry Fort Worth, he had to have the backing of the North Side.[19] While Shannon's political interpretation certainly no longer applies, a historical application definitely fits quite well. Fort Worth would not be what it is today — in size, in atmosphere, and in tourist business — were it not for North Fort Worth.

Folks who grew up on the North Side shortly after the turn of the century — and even as late as mid-century — knew that their part of town was unique. The Trinity River and the bluff on which downtown Fort Worth sprawls provided a geographic barrier, a dividing line that separated the North Side from the rest of Fort Worth, isolating it in a way that no other part of town experienced. While cattle barons crossed the river at night and went home to take a bath and wash away the smell of the stockyards, those who remained north of the river — the blue-collar, workingman's community — never escaped the "aroma" of the yards.

North Siders were defensive about their slaughterhouse industry and the part of town that housed it and them. Perhaps that same defensiveness made North Side high school sports teams more aggressive when they played the "rich" kids of Arlington Heights or the South Side. Whatever the cause, North Siders developed a camaraderie during the more than half a century that the stockyards and packing plants reigned as the biggest employers in Fort Worth. Residents were part of a vital, exuberant industry and the company town it spawned. They identified with their community and recognized others who shared the experience as comrades.

After mid-century, when the market began its decline, many people moved to other parts of the city, but they still thought of themselves as North Siders. Jenkins Garrett, lawyer and son of longtime minister for Rosen Heights Baptist Church, Jesse Garrett, claims that "once a North Sider, always a North Sider" and enjoys going back to his father's old church to teach a Sunday School class.[20]

Seventy-two-year-old Esmond Scarborough, who grew up next door to European immigrants, said, "We had a bond; it was an unspoken bond. We didn't know it at the time," Scarborough wrote.[21] "When I speak of North Fort Worth, I get a lump in my throat. It was truly a close-knit family of the best people on the earth."[22] He explained that their lower economic circumstances created humility in residents which in later life made them "forever thankful for all the blessings that the freedom of this country offered them."[23]

Charlie McCafferty called the feeling people have for the North Side a "community identity,"[24] and Jack Shannon feels a distinctive North Side spirit as well. He believes that the spirit is kept alive through people who grew up there or worked there. Dr. H. V. Helbing was his family physician, for example; now a North Side elementary school bears Helbing's name. "The Greines family, of course," Shannon remembered as he reminisced about their impact as doctors, lawyers, and businessmen. "The people of the North Side would come together when we had floods," he recalled. "People caring about people" expressed the concern of the close-knit community, according to Shannon.[25] Despite all the changes from livestock market and packing town to popular tourist haven, the spirit of North Fort Worth still lives.

Notes

CHAPTER 1

1. In 1856, the John Mitchell family purchased this land and it has since been known as the Mitchell Cemetery. Located behind the Fort Worth Grain Exchange at 2707 Decatur Avenue, it is one of the two oldest cemeteries in Tarrant County.
2. "Hog Packers Came Before 1900, Booming N. Side Fought Annexation," *Fort Worth Star-Telegram*, October 30, 1949, "North Side" Clipping File, University of Texas at Arlington, Special Collections, Arlington, Texas (hereafter cited as UTA Special Collections).
3. Charles Ellis Mitchell, "When Every Man Carried a Six Shooter," *In Old Fort Worth*, Mack Williams, ed. (Fort Worth: *The News-Tribune*, 1977), p. 46. Secondary sources conflict; some state that both men fired pistols.
4. "Tarrant's First Girl," in Mitchell Folder, Mary Daggett Lake Papers, Series IV, Box 2, p. 5, Fort Worth Public Library, Fort Worth (hereafter cited as MDL Papers).
5. Ibid.
6. Ibid., pp. 2-4.
7. C. C. Cummings Collection, *Fort Worth Star-Telegram*, Chapter 17, unnumbered pages, UTA Special Collections.
8. Mary Daggett Lake, "Founding of Fort Worth — Part Played by Taylor and Johnson Families," MDL Papers, Series IV, Box 3, pp. 1-2.

9. Ibid.
10. Howard W. Peak, "Uncle Jack Durrett, the Village Fiddler," *In Old Fort Worth*, p. 56.
11. Fort Worth and Tarrant County Federal Writer's Project, "Interview with John William Renfro," *Research Data*, vol. 2, p. 499 (Fort Worth Public Library).
12. *Fort Worth City Guide* in *Research Data*, vol. 1, p. 66.
13. Howard W. Peak, "An Episode of Old Fort Worth," *Research Data*, vol. 1, p. 207. Also "Charles Ellis Mitchell Biography," *Research Data*, vol. 5, p. 2000.
14. Peak, "An Episode of Old Fort Worth," *Research Data*, vol. 1, p. 208.
15. Ibid., pp. 208-209.
16. The creek was so named because marine fossils were found there.
17. E. M. (Bud) Daggett, "Tales by an Old-Timer," 1915, Cattle Industry in Texas Folder, MDL Papers, Series II, Box 1, p. 2. See also E. M. (Bud) Daggett, "Worked With Cattle for Over Sixty Years," 1920, p. 1, ibid.
18. Peak, "Old Water Mill," July 9, 1922, H. W. Peak Folder, MDL Papers, Series IV, Box 2, p. 2.
19. Names of Tarrant County Places, MDL Papers, Series II, Box 4, p. 5; also "Typed List of Historic Sites Visited March 5, 1949 by Mary Daggett Lake," MDL Papers, Series II, Box 3, p. 2.
20. "Fort Worth — Yesterday and Today," MDL Papers, State and Local History Series II, Box 4, p. 1. See also "Historic Walks" in Tarrant County History Folder, Ibid., p. 2, and "Names of Tarrant County Places," Ibid., p. 2..
21. "Tarrant's First Girl," in Mitchell Folder, MDL Papers, Series IV, Box 2, p. 5. Also "Landmarks Lie Under River Bluff," MDL Papers, Tarrant County History Folder.
22. Laura A. Daggett, "Reminiscences of My Life and Family," MDL Papers, Series II, Box 3, p. 18.
23. Ibid., p. 24.
24. Bud Daggett was named after his uncle, Ephraim Merrill Daggett who had come to Fort Worth to look the place over in 1849, later moving his family in 1854. Bud's father Charles Daggett brought his family in that year too, when Bud was only four.
25. Daggett, "Reminiscences," MDL Papers, Series II, Box 3, p. 27.
26. "About the Stockyards Today," *The Fort Worth Daily Live Stock Reporter*, July 11, 1904, p. 1.
27. Daggett, "Reminiscences," MDL Papers, Series II, Box 3, p. 45.

28. *Tarrant County Historic Resources Survey* (Fort Worth Historic Preservation Council for Tarrant County, Texas, 1988), p. 3.
29. Laura Haywood Brown, "Saga of North Fort Worth Baptist Story Community," *North Fort Worth News*, January 22, 1954, p. 10.
30. I.C. Bullard, *The Fort Worth Police Department*, 1901(UTA Special Collections), p. 4.

CHAPTER 2

1. Janie Reid, "The Thannisch Block Building, Fort Worth, Texas." Application for Official Texas Historical Marker on Stockyards Hotel, September 6, 1983, pp. 15-17. Application in Heritage Room, Tarrant County Junior College Library, Northeast Campus, Hurst, Texas.
2. It was located at the corner of North Main and Fourteenth where the brick M. G. Ellis School was later built.
3. Roy W. Haywood, "In Old Fort Worth: When the North Side Had Only 11 Homes," *The News-Tribune*, July 4, 1976, p. 16. (Recollections written in 1927.)
4. Ibid.
5. M. H. Moore served as principal of the M. G. Ellis School in 1911. He later became superintendent of Fort Worth schools. An elementary school at 1809 N.E. 36th Street in the North Side is named after him.
6. "M. G. Ellis, Sr., Laid to Rest," *Fort Worth Star-Telegram*, July 29, 1932, p. 5.
7. Peak, "Old Water Mill," July 9, 1922, H. W. Peak Folder, MDL Papers, Series IV, Box 2, p. 2.
8. Daggett, "Tales by an Old-Timer," Cattle Industry Folder, MDL Papers, Series II, Box 1, p. 2.
9. Duane Gage, Application for Texas Historical Marker for Eastern Cattle Trail, November 8, 1982, pp. 1, 4. Application in Heritage Room, Tarrant County Junior College, Northeast Campus, Hurst, Texas.
10. Interview with Reuben Jenkins, grandson of trail driver, Fort Worth, August 8, 1989.
11. For a full account of early attempts to bring meat-packing plants to Fort Worth see J'Nell L. Pate, *Livestock Legacy: The Fort Worth Stockyards, 1887-1987* (College Station: Texas A & M University Press, 1988), pp. 12-16.

12. Charter No. 3402, Fort Worth Union Stock Yards Company, filed July 26, 1887, Office of Secretary of State, Austin, Texas.

13. Bullard, *Fort Worth Police Department*, Chapter 17, p. 3.

14. Holloway Folder, MDL Papers, Series IV, Box 2.

15. "An Electrical Railway Ten Miles Long Will Soon Be Built," *The Weekly Gazette*, Fort Worth, February 1, 1889, in *Research Data*, vol. 5, pp. 1725-1726.

16. Bud Shrake, "Old Days on Mule Cart Took Madden Through 'Hell's Acre,' " *Fort Worth Press*, September 1, 1957, p. 11.

17. Claire Eyrich, "Trolleys Clank Gently Into City's Heritage," *Fort Worth Star-Telegram*, August 15, 1965, Sect. 2, p. 1.

18. Charter No. 4581, The Fort Worth Packing Company, filed April 30, 1890, Office of Secretary of State, Austin, Texas. Directors included John R. Hoxie, E. B. Harrold, John Peter Smith, Joe C. McCarthy, M. G. Ellis, A. T. Byers, and R. H. Sellars.

19. Lila Bunch Race, *Pioneer Fort Worth, Texas: The Life, Time and Families of South Tarrant County* (Dallas: Taylor Publishing Co., 1976), pp. 26-27.

20. Written transcript of interview with Verner S. Wardlaw, 1861-1924, "The History of the Packing Plant Industry in Fort Worth," 1915 (Copy in author's possession), p. 4.

21. Board of Directors Meeting, April 24, 1893, *Corporate Record*, Fort Worth Stock Yards Company, vol. 1, pp. 27-28. The total price paid for both the stockyards and the packing plant was $350,066.66. Board of Directors Meeting, August 8, 1893, *Corporate Record*, vol. 1, p. 36.

22. Proceedings of the Twenty-first Annual Convention of the Cattle Raisers Association of Texas, March 9-10, 1897, in San Antonio, p. 71. See also Proceedings, 1893-1899, at Waggoner Library, Texas and Southwestern Cattle Raisers Association, Fort Worth.

23. C. C. French, "The History of a Great Fort Worth Institution: The Southwestern Exposition and Fat Stock Show," C. C. French Manuscripts in *Research Data*, vol. 62, p. 24582.

24. Sam Smith, *Things I Remember About Early Days in History of Fort Worth* (Fort Worth: River Oaks Printing, 1965), p. 11.

25. "For Big Packery," *Texas Stock Journal*, June 12, 1901, p. 1.

26. Copy of a contract between Fort Worth Stock Yards Company and Swift and Company, January 25, 1902, unmarked folder, Gary Havard Personal Collection, Fort Worth.

27. "The Bonus Raised," *Texas Stock Journal*, October 8, 1901 , p. 1.

28. "Both Packing Houses Now Assured," *The Fort Worth Register*, October 8, 1901, p. 1.

29. Board of Directors Meeting, January 25, 1902, *Corporate Record*, Fort Worth Stock Yards Company, vol. 1, pp. 217-18.

30. "Col. H. C. Holloway Dies At His Home," *Fort Worth Record*, April 29, 1905, Holloway Folder, MDL Papers, Series IV, Box 2.

31. "Balloon Ascension at Stockyards in Park Tomorrow Night By Moonlight," *Fort Worth Telegram*, August 21, 1902, p. 8.

32. "The Great Packing Plants," *The Texas Farm Journal*, March 10, 1903, p. 2. Also "City and County," *The Fort Worth Daily Live Stock Reporter*, February 7, 1903, p. 1. This Exchange Building stands today at 131 East Exchange Avenue.

33. "City and County," *The Fort Worth Daily Live Stock Reporter*, February 21, 1903, p. 1. Also "Gov. Lanham Can't Come," ibid., February 26, 1903, p. 1.

34. "Opening of the Big Plants," *The Fort Worth Daily Live Stock Reporter*, March 4, 1903, p. 1. Also "Fat Stock Show Begins," ibid., March 5, 1903, p. 1, and "Around the Stockyards," ibid., March 9, 1903, p. 1.

35. "Get Down to Business," *The Citizen*, November 20, 1903, p. 1.

36. Janie Reid, Application for Official Texas Historical Marker on Stockyards Hotel, September 6, 1983, pp. 13-14.

37. "One of the Big Markets," *The Fort Worth Daily Live Stock Reporter*, February 6, 1905, p. 1. Also "Fort Worth Receipts for 1909," Ibid., January 1, 1910, p. 1.

38. Hollace Weiner, "Packed with Memories," *Fort Worth Star-Telegram*, May 14, 1988, part 2, sect. 1, pp. 25-26.

39. Collective interview with Marian Butler, Dorothy Franklin Shear, and Ailene and J. E. Cavender, Fort Worth, August 18, 1989.

40. Weiner, "Packed with Memories," p. 25.

41. Ibid.

42. Collective interview with Butler, Shear, and Cavender. A junior high school, now middle school, was later named after J. P. Elder, a superintendent at Swift.

43. "Commerce," *Fort Worth Record*, July 29, 1915, in *Research Data*, vol. 21, pp. 8218-19; *Annual Report, 1917*, Fort Worth Stockyards Company Collection.

44. *Annual Report*, 1917, Fort Worth Stock Yards Company, Fort Worth Stock Yards Company Collection, University of North Texas Archives, Denton, Texas.

45. Max Baker, "Historic District Sought for Grand Avenue Area," *Fort Worth Star-Telegram*, sect. 1, January 1, 1988, pp. 21-22.

46. Advertising Clippings, W. L. Pier Correspondence, Fort Worth Stock Yards Company Collection.

47. Comparison of Receipts and Disposition of Livestock, 1964-1981, Fort Worth Stock Yards Company, Fort Worth.
48. Interview with Butler, Shear, and Cavender. The Swift plant in Fort Worth did not strike from 1937 until the plant closed.
49. "Parks for Diamond Hill Won by Civic League," *Fort Worth Star-Telegram*, October 30, 1949, "Diamond Hill" Clipping File, *Fort Worth Star-Telegram* Collection, UTA Special Collections.
50. Janie Reid, "Application for Official Historical Marker for Trail Drivers' Park, 1984," pp. 4-11. See also "Old Trail Driver Park," p. 1, manuscript in History of Fort Worth Parks Folder, MDL Papers, Series V. See also Lake, "Typed List of Historic Sites Visited March 5, 1949," MDL Papers, Series II. Box 3, p. 2. A stream named Gilmore's Branch, after Seaborn Gilmore, runs through Trail Drivers' Park.

CHAPTER 3

1. "Minutes," City Council Meeting, City of North Fort Worth (1902-1909 volume), February 28, 1905, p. 100. They cited 4,567 inhabitants.
2. *Tarrant County Historic Resources Survey*, p. 4.
3. "Minutes," December 9, 1902, p. 1.
4. Smith, *Things I Remember*, p. 3.
5. "North Fort Worth Council," *The Fort Worth Daily Live Stock Reporter*, February 11, 1903, p. 1.
6. "Mayor Farmer Has a Gavel," *The Fort Worth Daily Live Stock Reporter*, February 11, 1903, p. 1.
7. "Minutes," December 23, 1903, p. 27.
8. Ibid., pp. 41-42.
9. Ibid., March 11, 1908, p. 310.
10. "Heart Attack Fatal To Rosen," *Fort Worth Star-Telegram*, December 21, 1932, "Rosen A-Z" Clipping File, *Fort Worth Star-Telegram* Collection, UTA Special Collections.
11. Ibid.
12. Esmond Scarborough, "Reminiscences of the North Side" (author's collection, obtained from Mr. Scarborough), p. 59. The present streets which form boundaries of the first Rosen Heights Addition are Gould Avenue on the east, Twenty-third on the south, Twenty-eighth on the north, and Roosevelt on the west.
13. "Sam Rosen Made A Modest Start, He Now Owns a Fort Worth Suburb," *The Fort Worth Telegram*, October 30, 1904, p. 17. Clipping borrowed

from Sam Rosen and Ron Rosen, grandsons. See also "City and County," *The Fort Worth Daily Live Stock Reporter*, August 10, 1903, p. 4.

14. Rosen Heights Advertisement, *The Fort Worth Daily Live Stock Reporter*, June 27, 1903, p. 2.

15. Rosen Heights Advertisement, *The Fort Worth Daily Live Stock Reporter*, June 9, 1903, p. 4.

16. "Minutes," April 19, 1904, p. 36.

17. Interview with Louise Cloud, Fort Worth, August 27, 1989.

18. From a plat map in Rosen Heights Land Company Office, 312 Northwest Twenty-fifth Street. Phase II went all the way to Sherman Street on the north, or what was the old Sansom Ranch which makes up the present city of Sansom Park.

19. Xeroxed pages in Rosen family files, p. 33.

20. Smith, *Things I Remember*, p. 3.

21. "Sam Rosen Made a Modest Start," p. 17.

22. The North Side Exchange eventually became Prospect, one of four exchanges in the greater Fort Worth area. The downtown Fort Worth Exchange was Lamar; Rosedale was for the east side, and Pershing for Arlington Heights. These exchanges were in place by the 1920s. Interview with Cloud.

23. Advertisement, *The Fort Worth Daily Live Stock Reporter*, May 19, 1903, p. 4.

24. "North Fort Worth Improvements," *The Fort Worth Daily Live Stock Reporter*, January 28, 1903, p. 1. Also Hollace Weiner, "Pioneer Was on the Right Track," *Fort Worth Star-Telegram*, sect. B. June 23, 1986, pp. 1-3.

25. Scarborough, "Reminiscences." Also interview with Sam Rosen and Ron Rosen (grandsons), Fort Worth, January 10, 1986.

26. Ibid. Sam Rosen died in 1932, suffering a stroke sometime prior to his death.

27. Eyrich, "Trolleys Clank Gently Into City's Heritage."

28. Interview with Cloud.

29. Ibid., August 20, 1989.

30. Ibid. Louise married Francis R. Cloud, the son of well-to-do laundry owner, Ernest T. Cloud.

31. "Minutes," March 9, 1909, p. 369. Also "Hog Packers Came Before 1900, Booming N. Side Fought Annexation," *Fort Worth Star-Telegram*, October 30, 1949.

32. "Minutes," Niles City Council, February 25, 1911, vol. 1, p. 2. Judge's order copied in minute book.

33. Janie Reid, "Niles City, Texas," History essay accompanying

Historical Marker Application for Texas Historical Marker, 1980. Located in Heritage Room, Tarrant County Junior College, Northeast Campus, Hurst, Texas. In 1982 a Niles City Historical Marker was dedicated at the Stockyards. Descendants of Louville Niles attended the ceremony.

34. Ibid., p. 6. The boundaries of Niles City were Marine Creek on the west, Twenty-ninth Street on the north, Harding on the east, and the Trinity River on the south.
35. Ibid., p. 4.
36. "Minutes," Niles City Council, December 16, 1911, vol. 1, p. 18. Also "Site is Purchased for Niles City Hall," *North Fort Worth Sunday News*, November 26, 1911, p. 1. The five aldermen elected to serve with Carson were M. V. Simms, J. Childs, N. L. Atherton, Fred Harr, and W. H. Griffith. W. L. Johnson was city marshall.
37. Williams, *In Old Fort Worth*, p. 33. It operated under various editors for the next seventy-four years, ceasing publication in 1985 after being absorbed by a chain of suburban newspapers.
38. Reid, "Niles City, Texas," pp. 1-2. Also "Minutes," Niles City Council, April 25, 1921, vol. 1. pp. 212-13.
39. "Minutes," Niles City Council, November 3, 1922, vol. 1, p. 237.
40. "Niles Adds 30 Million to City's Assets," *Fort Worth Star-Telegram*, August 11, 1923. Also Niles City File, *Fort Worth Star-Telegram* Reference Library, Fort Worth.

CHAPTER 4

1. Jethro K. Lieberman, *Are Americans Extinct?* (New York: Walker Co., 1968), pp. 23, 25.
2. "Social Life," *Fort Worth Star-Telegram*, November 25, 1913, in *Research Data*, vol. 36, p. 14275.
3. Lieberman, *Are Americans Extinct?* p. 26.
4. Melvin Steinfield, ed., *Cracks in the Melting Pot: Racism and Discrimination in American History* (Beverly Hills, California: Glencoe Press, 1970), p. xv.
5. Lou Ostrako, "As I Remember," Pamphlet (Fort Worth: Privately printed, May, 1990), p. 33.
6. "Social Life," p. 14272.
7. The Department of Immigration classified "Slavs" as Poles, Slovaks, Croatians, Slovenians, Ruthenians, Russniak, Moravians, Bohemians, Bulgarians, Serbians, Montenegrins, Russians, Dalmatians, Bosnians and Herzegovinians. See George M. Stephenson, *A History of American*

Immigration, 1820-1924 (New York: Russell & Russell, Inc., 1964), p. 87.

8. Collective interview with Butler, Shear, and Cavender.

9. Interview with Edwin Cohen, grandson of Meyer and Sarah Greines, Fort Worth, January 27, 1986.

10. Collective interview, Butler, Shear, and Cavender.

11. Interview with workers at Greines Furniture Store, Fort Worth, January 22, 1986.

12. Scarborough, "Reminiscences," p. 21.

13. T. Herman Muller, "Germans 1900-1918," in *Research Data*, vol. 1, p. 1.

14. "Fort Worth — Yesterday and Today," MDL Papers, Series I, Box 4, p. 1.

15. Muller, "Germans," pp. 3-4.

16. Lake, "Landmarks Lie Under River Bluff," MDL Papers, pp. 1-2.

17. Rosemary Woods, "Contemporary Fraternity Within the North Fort Worth Czechoslovakian Community and Its Background," unpublished research paper written for a University of North Texas geography course in May 1978, pp. 5, 10. Obtained from Czech Community Sokol Hall.

18. Joan Lamb, "A Conspectus of Change In the Czechoslovakian Settlement of Northside Fort Worth, From 1900 to 1979," unpublished research paper obtained from Czech Community Sokol Hall, p. 3. Sokol literally means "falcon" and represents swiftness, vigor, strength and daring. See Clinton Machann and James W. Mendl, *Krásná Amerika: A Story of the Texas Czechs, 1851-1939* (Austin: Eakin Press, 1983), p. 91. Since 1989, Sokol has re-emerged in Czechoslovakia.

19. V. A. Svreck, editor-translator, *A History of the Czech-Moravian Catholic Communities of Texas* (Waco: Texian Press, 1974), p. 82.

20. Scarborough, "Reminiscences"; also, interview with Mrs. Rudolph "Rudy" Wruble (Millie Haba), Fort Worth, July 8, 1992.

21. Charles H. Mindel and Robert W. Habenstein, eds., *Ethnic Families in America: Patterns and Variations* (New York: Elsevier Publishing Co., 1976), p. 169.

22. "Greeks in Fort Worth," *Fort Worth City Guide* in *Research Data*, vol. 46, p. 18182.

23. Interview with Mary Sparto, Fort Worth, August 22, 1992.

24. Interview with Mrs. Steve (Georgia) Pappajohn, Fort Worth, August 22, 1992.

25. Interview with Carnation "Connie" Salicos Samaras, daughter of George Salicos, Fort Worth, August 31, 1992.

26. "Our Parish At a Glance," p. 1, xeroxed article obtained at St. Demetrios Greek Orthodox Church, Twenty-first and Jacksboro Highway, Fort Worth. Also, Mindel and Habenstein, eds., *Ethnic Families in America*, pp. 169, 171. As of this writing, a split between parishioners at St. Demetrios over the employment of Pastor Theodore Bita threatened to close the church. See, "Legal Fight Shuts Doors of Church," *Fort Worth Star-Telegram*, February 22, 1994.

27. Interview with Hyman and Maxine Jacobson, Fort Worth, December 1, 1986.

28. "How 'Calf fries' came to Fort Worth," *Fort Worth Star-Telegram*, August 6, 1978, "North Side" File, *Fort Worth Star-Telegram* Reference Library.

29. Ibid.

30. Ibid. Riscky's restaurant later opened in the building.

31. Johnny Cabluck, communication with the author, Spring 1992. Also Orville Hancock, "Hard work leads to life of fulfillment," *Fort Worth Star-Telegram*, January 25, 1989, clipping file of Esmond Scarborough, loaned to author. The original Riscky's Barbecue was located at 2314 Azle Avenue.

32. Juliet George Dees, "The Clinton Avenue Baptist Church for Slavic People: An Emigrant Institution in Fort Worth 1920-1961," unpublished research paper, Texas Christian University, 1987, p. 1-2.

33. Ibid., pp. 1.

34. Ibid., p. 11.

35. Ibid., p. 13.

36. Untitled story by Johnny Cabluck, privately printed, 1988, pp. 10-11. Copy in author's possession.

37. The store, owned by Charlie Goldstein, was in the 1000 block of Houston.

38. Cabluck, untitled story.

39. "Social Life," p. 14275.

40. Ostrako, "As I Remember," p. 26.

41. Samuel Joseph, *Jewish Immigration to the United States From 1881 to 1910* (New York; Arno Press and *The New York Times*, 1969; originally published 1914), p. 157.

42. Lieberman, *Are Americans Extinct?*; also Scarborough, "Reminiscences," p. 22.

CHAPTER 5

1. Reid, "The Thannisch Block Building, Fort Worth, Texas."

2. Ibid., pp. 4-5. In 1982 heirs of Mr. Thannisch sold the building to Tom Yater of Alvarado and Marshall Young of Cleburne.

3. "New Cold Storage Plant," *The Fort Worth Daily Live Stock Reporter*, August 27, 1904, p. 1.

4. Interview with Rita Renfro, Fort Worth, August 9, 1989.

5. George Smith, "W.O 'Pinky' Chenault, 72, Restaurant Owner, Mason," obituary *Fort Worth Star-Telegram*, August 29, 1990, Scarborough Clipping File. Chenault's restaurant on Jacksboro Highway is still in operation, but the name changed when his ex-wife obtained it as a part of a divorce settlement. It is now Vivian Courtney's Restaurant, 5915 Lake Worth Boulevard.

6. Interview with Rex and Lois Brewer, Fort Worth, January 16, 1986.

7. Interview with Esmond Scarborough, Azle, February 8, 1992.

8. Ibid.

9. Ibid.

10. Roach originally located his insurance business where the bar area in Cattlemen's Steak House presently exists. At one time Roach owned the Farmer's Daughter, Cattlemen's in downtown Dallas, Cattlemen's Preston Center, and Cattlemen's Arlington. By 1986 he had sold or closed all but the original restaurant on the North Side.

11. Advertisement, *Fort Worth Star-Telegram*, 1909, reproduced in "Texas Siftings," *Fort Worth Star-Telegram*, December 11, 1988, sect. 3. p. 1.

12. Interview with Dottie Moore, Fort Worth, September 24, 1989. After Mr. Vinnedge died in 1944, Morton Foods occupied the building for a time. It later sat vacant and run-down until Jess Cole and Bruce Baird bought it in 1985 and spent $1.6 million to renovate it as a modern office building.

13. This Courthouse Market is not the one two blocks east of the courthouse on Belknap Street; the one that exists today began in 1940 as Bill Skelton's Grocery. The name was changed to Courthouse Market in 1963 when Harold Anderson bought it. The Courthouse Market in which Jack Ellis worked during the 1920s and 1930s was located near Leonard's Department Store on Houston Street.

14. Interview with Jackie and Jack Ellis, Fort Worth, January 7, 1986. In October 1991, the Ellises sold to Hammons Products of Stockton, Missouri. Brian Hammons now serves as president, but the Ellis Pecan name is retained.

15. Gail Beckham, "Three Firms Flourish/Hand-Made Saddles Are Big Business Here," *Fort Worth Star-Telegram*, March 6, 1960, *Fort Worth Star-Telegram* Clipping File, UTA Special Collections.

16. Ibid.

17. Interview with Wilson Franklin, Fort Worth, January 8, 1986.

18. Interview with Richard Allen, Fort Worth, June 22, 1987. Also interview with Louise Barnhart, Fort Worth, June 25, 1987. The two-story, red-brick building at 2350 N. Main which was the 1908 site of Lewis Furniture and Stoves is still standing. In fact, on its south side can still be seen the letters, "ure and stoves."

19. Scarborough, "Reminiscences," pp. 105-106.

20. Ibid., p. 102.

21. Amy Keen, "Barbering pair head for retirement," *Fort Worth Star-Telegram*, 1984, Clipping file of Esmond Scarborough.

22. Interview with Jack and Pat Shannon, Fort Worth, January 8, 1986. Also "Biographical Sketch of County Judge S. D. Shannon," *Fort Worth Star-Telegram* Clipping File, UTA Special Collections.

23. Oliver Shannon, "North Side 75 Years Ago," *In Old Fort Worth*, p. 93.

24. Interview with Jack and Pat Shannon. S. D. Shannon was killed in an auto accident in Scotland, Archer County Texas, when he was on his way to visit his daughter in Wichita Falls in September 1946. He was seventy-nine years old. Editorial "S. Dave Shannon," *Fort Worth Star-Telegram*, September 24, 1946, *Fort Worth Star-Telegram* Clipping file "Shannon, S. D." in UTA Special Collections.

25. Scarborough, "Reminiscences," p. 47.

26. Ibid.

27. Ibid.

28. Ibid., pp. 37-38.

29. Ibid., p. 101.

30. "Hobbs Starts 50th Year," *Fort Worth Star-Telegram*, 1976, Scarborough Clipping file.

31. According to a Dallas newspaper story in the early 1870s before the railroad arrived, Fort Worth was such a sleepy little town that a panther had been seen walking down Main Street. Some say it even took a nap. Fort Worth citizens adopted the name "Panther City" in retaliation to the Dallas put-down and wore it proudly.

32. Interview with A. M. Pate, Jr., Fort Worth, January 10, 1986.

CHAPTER 6

1. Jack Gordon, "Arkansas Man Tours Texas: Learns Why Cowtown is Different," *Fort Worth Press*, November 17, 1948, p. 16, Clipping in Tarrant County History Clippings, 1926-1950, MDL Papers.

2. "Two Killed, Two Are Hurt As Stock Yards Bank Robbed," *Fort Worth Star-Telegram*, August 9, 1930, pp. 1, 4.

3. Interview with Charlie McCafferty, Fort Worth, October 29, 1979.

4. "Colonel H. C. Holloway," MDL Papers, Series IV, Box 2, back of p. 6.

5. Ruby Schmidt, ed., *Fort Worth & Tarrant County: A Historic Guide*, (Fort Worth: Texas Christian University Press, 1984), pp. 31-32.

6. Smith, *Things I Remember*, p. 1.

7. Mary Daggett Lake, "Rich Historical Material Abounds in Tarrant County: Old Landmarks Designated," Tarrant County History Manuscripts, MDL Papers. See also Jim Marrs, "Those who try can find the history of Fort Worth," *Fort Worth Star-Telegram*, undated clipping files of Nelda Cook, Fort Worth.

8. "City and County," *The Fort Worth Daily Livestock Reporter*, February 7, 1903, p. 1.

9. The first time that labor violence occurred was the Great Southwest strike in 1886 in which Jay Gould's Southern Pacific Railroad workers tried to prevent the trains from moving. Jim Courtright, a former law officer, intervened.

10. "Weapon May Prove Owner Took Part in Rouse Lynching," *Fort Worth Star-Telegram*, December 12, 1921, p. 1-2. Also "Labor," *Fort Worth Star-Telegram*, October 1, 1922, in *Research Data*, vol. 32, p. 12743.

11. William E. Leuchtenberg, *Perils of Prosperity, 1914-1932* (Chicago: University of Chicago Press, 1958), p. 127.

12. Daniel Lamb, "Northside Fort Worth: An Historical Summary," mimeographed pages obtained at North Side High School, p. 2.

13. "Klansmen Initiate Class of 932 Here In Weird Ceremony," *Fort Worth Star-Telegram*, May 27, 1922, "Ku Klux Klan" Clipping File, *Fort Worth Star-Telegram* Collection, UTA Special Collections.

14. Ibid., also "Klan In Letter Declares It Is Lawful and Here To Stay," *Fort Worth Star-Telegram*, January 8, 1922, "Ku Klux Klan" Clipping Files in *Fort Worth Star-Telegram* Collection, UTA Special Collections.

15. "Klansmen Initiate Class."

16. Some claimed that the Fort Worth Klan membership numbered eight to ten thousand. "Ku Klux Klan," *Fort Worth Press*, July 1, 1924, in *Research Data*, vol. 13, p. 5001. Also "Klansmen Initiate Class."

17. "Probe of Klan Hall Fire Starts," *Fort Worth Star-Telegram*, November 6, 1924, p. 1.

18. Ibid., p. 4.

19. Ibid.

20. "Injunction Sought in Baptist Auditorium Dispute," *Fort Worth Star-Telegram*, November 6, 1924, p. 1. The Klan apparently was not considered the "bad" group in the 1920s that later generations would so judge it. Contemporary newspaper articles gave the impression that it was just another civic organization.

21. W. G. Byrne, "Klan Minstrel Turns 'Em Away; Scores Hit; 'On Again' at Church," *Fort Worth Star-Telegram*, November 8, 1924, p. 2.

22. In May, 1927, someone tossed a note through a window in downtown Fort Worth where Klansmen were meeting. It said, "We will give you 30 days to get out or we will use twice as much dynamite on this building as we did on the Klan Hall. We are getting tired of you getting into other people's business." It was signed "The Blacks." Most observers believed that the authors of the note were trying to blame blacks and perhaps were not black themselves. "Threat Made To Dynamite Hall of Klan," *Fort Worth Star-Telegram*, May 20, 1927, "Ku Klux Klan" Clipping File, *Fort Worth Star-Telegram* Collection, UTA Special Collections.

23. The Klan building fell into disuse for a time, but by the late 1930s promoters of wrestling on the North Side rehabilitated it. They placed approximately 2,000 seats on inclines constructed around a stage in the center of the building. After wrestling moved to the North Side Coliseum, the former Klan hall became a storage warehouse for a downtown department store. Then in 1947 the Ellis Pecan Company purchased it; the company still uses it as their main offices and warehouse.

24. Scarborough, "Reminiscences," p. 36.

25. Ibid., p. 37.

26. Ibid.

27. Interview with Scarborough.

28. Scarborough, "Reminiscences," p. 105.

29. Ibid., pp. 108-109.

30. Collective interview with Butler, Shear, and Cavender.

CHAPTER 7

1. The free movies at Marine Park were for whites only. Even Hispanics who lived east of North Main Street were not welcome west of Main in the 1920s, 1930s and 1940s. See Chapter 10.

2. Laura Haywood Brown, "Saga of North Fort Worth Baptist Story Community," *North Fort Worth News*, January 22, 1954, p. 10, in History of Church Folder, at North Fort Worth Baptist Church, 5801 North Freeway, Fort Worth.

3. The church gradually expanded until — in 1966 — it included the entire block. Leon McBeth, *Victory Through Prayer: A History of Rosen Heights Baptist Church, 1906-1966* (Fort Worth: Rosen Heights Baptist Church, 1966), pp. 3-8.

4. Ibid., pp. 23, 25. Garrett's son, Jenkins, did become a lawyer. Prominent in civic affairs, he is a well-known local philanthropist.

5. Moore eventually became principal of North Side High School.

6. Telephone interview with office staff, North Side Church of Christ, Fort Worth, February 5, 1986. In 1970 the church started a Spanish-speaking congregation, Iglesia de Cristo, which began meeting at Twentieth and Lincoln streets. "This Week's Church; 12 Started Church In School Building," *Fort Worth Star-Telegram*, May 19, 1956, in "North Side Church of Christ" Clipping File, *Fort Worth Star-Telegram* Collection, UTA Special Collections.

7. The first local Catholic church — St. Patrick's — was built in 1890.

8. *Our Celebration: All Saints Catholic Church, Fort Worth, Texas* (South Hackensack, New Jersey: Custombook, Inc., 1977), p. 21.

9. Interview with Ursula Strittmatter, Fort Worth, January 14, 1986.

10. In 1951 the church merged with the John Knox Presbyterian and moved to the River Oaks area. *Tarrant County Historic Resources Survey*, p. 38.

11. "Church to Observe Tenth Anniversary," *Fort Worth Star-Telegram*, November 25, 1938, and "Presbyterians Will Observe Anniversary," *Fort Worth Star-Telegram*, November 25, 1953, both in *Fort Worth Star-Telegram* Collection, UTA Special Collections.

12. "North Fort Worth Church Starts on New Sanctuary," *Fort Worth Star-Telegram*, April 11, 1956, *Fort Worth Star-Telegram* Clipping File, "North Fort Worth," UTA Special Collections.

13. *Tarrant County Historic Resources Survey*, p. 37.

14. Roy W. Haywood, "In Old Fort Worth: When the North Side Had Only 11 homes," *In Old Fort Worth*, p. 16.

15. "Parks," *Fort Worth Record*, April 17, 1910, in *Research Data*, vol. 20, p. 7683.

16. "Parks," *Fort Worth Press*, June 10, 1927, in *Research Data*, vol. 17, p. 6639.

17. Cabluck, letter to author, Spring 1992.

18. "Government," *Fort Worth Press*, June 15, 1926, in *Research Data*, vol. 16, p. 6270.
19. Interview with Renfro.
20. "Old Rosen Home on North Side Will Come Down," *Fort Worth Star-Telegram*, March 28, 1941, *Fort Worth Star-Telegram* Clipping File "Rosen A-Z," UTA Special Collections. Also "Heart Attack Fatal To Rosen," *Fort Worth Star-Telegram*, December 21, 1932.
21. Cabluck, letter to author, December 12, 1989. Also Oliver Shannon, "North Side 75 Years Ago," *In Old Fort Worth*, p. 93.
22. Ibid.
23. Interview with Rosen and Rosen.
24. "Amusement," *Fort Worth Star-Telegram*, June 17, 1933, in *Research Data*, vol. 38, pp. 15134-35.
25. Tidball's bank was not the later North Fort Worth Bank; that bank did not open until 1941.
26. "New Isis Theater History Recalled on Birthday Eve," *Fort Worth Star-Telegram*, March 26, 1946, *Fort Worth Star-Telegram* Clipping File "New Isis Theater," UTA Special Collections.
27. Interview with Winston Sparks, Fort Worth, May 12, 1983.
28."New Isis Theatre History Recalled On Birthday Eve."
29. *Tarrant County Historic Resources Survey*, p. 75.
30. "1935 Saw Start of Boys Club, " *Fort Worth Star-Telegram*, October 30, 1949, *Fort Worth Star-Telegram* Clipping File "North Fort Worth Boys Club," UTA Special Collections.
31. "Church Gymnasium Becomes Haven for 205 Boys of Club," *Fort Worth Star-Telegram*, February 2, 1935, *Fort Worth Star-Telegram* Clipping File, UTA Special Collections.
32. Christopher Evans, "Personalities; For the Boys," *Fort Worth Star-Telegram* (no date) in Scarborough Clipping file.
33. Interview with Joe Cordova, Fort Worth, June 30, 1992.
34. Scarborough, "Reminiscences," p. 29.
35. "Military Escort Will Be Provided for Col. Roosevelt," *The Fort Worth Record*, March 11, 1911, p. 1. Also "Roosevelt Will Be Guest of Fat Stock Show Today," *The Fort Worth Record*, March 14, 1911, p. 1.
36. Interview with Louise Barnhart, Fort Worth, June 25, 1987.
37. "Neither Stock Show Nor Market Affected By Fire," *The Fort Worth Record*, March 15, 1911, p. 1.
38. "Roosevelt's Stay Short But Snappy, Delivers Address," *The Fort Worth Record*, March 15, 1911, p. 12.
39. Ibid. Roosevelt referred to a 1906 wolf hunt in the Indian Territory

hosted by Burk Burnett and W. T. Waggoner for the former president.

40. Ibid.

41. Smith, *Things I Remember*, p. 11. Also interview with Louise Cloud, Fort Worth, August 20, 1989.

42. *Fort Worth Star-Telegram* publisher Amon G. Carter was instrumental in obtaining New Deal public works funds for constructing the coliseum-auditorium complex on Lancaster Street as a project of the Texas Centennial celebration; some state money also was appropriated. Carter also successfully urged that the facility be named for his friend Will Rogers, who had been killed in an airplane crash in 1935.

43. Kathie Brown, "North Side Coliseum Tradition Continuing," *Fort Worth Star-Telegram*, May 27, 1974, n.p.

CHAPTER 8

1. "Biography of Captain B. B. Paddock," in *Research Data*, vol. 4, p. 1497.

2. Julia Kathryn Garrett, *Fort Worth: A Frontier Triumph* (Austin: The Encino Press, 1972,) pp. 334-35.

3. "Biography of Captain B. B. Paddock," in *Research Data*, p. 1498.

4. Duane Gage, "The Paddock Viaduct," Essay accompanying Historical Marker Application December 17, 1979, pp. 1-3. Located in Heritage Room, Learning Resources Center, Tarrant County Junior College, Northeast Campus. Hurst, Texas.

5. Ibid., p. 4.

6. "Texas Cattle," *The Fort Worth Democrat*, April 21, 1875, p. 3.

7. Interview with Louise Cloud. Later repairs and renovations were made on the bridge, and the streetcar tracks were removed in the 1940s.

8. "Plant Closing Not to Affect Gulf Activities," *Fort Worth Star-Telegram*, March 26, 1954, *Fort Worth Star-Telegram* Clipping File, "Gulf Oil Corp." UTA Special Collections.

9. *Fort Worth City Directory, 1927* (Dallas: Morrison and Fourmy Directory Co., Inc., 1927), p. 7.

10. *FAA Southwest Region Recollections and Reflections* A Bicentennial History Project Prepared and Distributed by the Public Affairs Office (1976), p. 1. The Southwest Region office of the Federal Aviation Administration at 4400 Blue Mound Road is located on the site

where the U.S. Navy conducted experiments in separating helium from natural gas.

11. "New U.S. Helium Plant Will Cost $2,060,800," *Fort Worth Star-Telegram*, December 20, 1928, *Fort Worth Star-Telegram* Clipping File, UTA Special Collections. The article told of the new plant to be constructed in Amarillo after the Fort Worth plant closed.

12. "Science and Invention, Texas As the 'Home of Helium,' " *The Literary Digest*, October 11, 1919, pp. 23-24.

13. "City Big Airship Base for U.S." *Fort Worth Press*, September 13, 1924, in *Research Data*, vol. 13, p. 5119; also "Aviation," *The Fort Worth Press*, November 19, 1923, *Research Data*, vol. 15, p. 5708.

14. "Points of Interest," *The Fort Worther*, January, 1954, p. 8, MDL Papers. Also "Fort Worth's Historical Airport Began in Grassy Cow Pastures," *Cowtown Trails*, March 1984, p. 17.

15. Mabel Gouldy, "Pioneer Saw Field Develop From Pasture to Airport," *Fort Worth Star-Telegram*, April 17, 1960, *Fort Worth Star-Telegram* Clipping File "Meacham Field," UTA Special Collections.

16. "Aviation," *Fort Worth Star-Telegram*, July 21, 1929, in *Research Data*, vol. 39, p. 15308.

17. Interview with Myra Harris, Retirement Office, City of Fort Worth, Fort Worth, June 22, 1992. When Fuller arrived in 1925, he was the only Fort Worth resident employed in aviation. In 1957, he was one of thousands (including employees of manufacturing plants and those stationed at Carswell). Don Williams, "Meacham Spruces Up Service To Boost 'Executive' Business," *Fort Worth Star-Telegram*, November 10, 1957, *Fort Worth Star-Telegram* Clipping File "Meacham Field," UTA Special Collections.

18. *Research Data*, vol. 52, p. 20713.

19. "Fort Worth's Historical Airport Began in Grassy Cow Pasture," *Cowtown Trails*, p. 17.

20. "Aviation," *Fort Worth Press*, September 23, 1927, in *Research Data*, vol. 18, pp. 6824-6825.

21. *Fort Worth Star-Telegram*, September 26, 1927, in *Research Data*, vol. 7, p. 2447.

22. Mack Williams, "The Day Lindy Came to Town," *In Old Fort Worth*, pp. 122-23. Even long after its importance was eclipsed by the near-by Dallas-Fort Worth International Airport, Meacham Field still hosts an occasional celebrity. While campaigning for president in 1980, Ronald Reagan landed at Meacham and spoke to a large crowd in a hangar. Bill Clinton also spoke at the field during his presidential campaign in 1992.

23."Meacham Airport remains Ft. Worth center of general aviation activity," *Times-Record Progress* (1991), p. 10.

24. *Fort Worth Star-Telegram*, September 26, 1929, in *Research Data*, vol. 7, p. 2448.

25. "Endurance Aviator Airsick: Pilot Drops Message Asking Medicine and 2 Parachutes. Reg Robbins Takes Ill; Ship Will Be Refueled Again Later Today," *Fort Worth Press*, May 20, 1929, in *Research Data*, vol. 19, pp. 7388-7389.

26. Ibid., p. 7388.

27. Ibid., pp. 7389-7391.

28. "Aviation," *Fort Worth Star-Telegram*, May 27, 1929, in *Research Data*, vol. 39, pp. 15301-302.

29. "Fort Worth's Historical Airport Began in Grassy Cow Pasture," p. 17. Also *Fort Worth Star-Telegram*, May 26, 1929, sect. 2, p. 1. An airplane taking off from Meacham Field set another record of sorts in December 1946 when the world's first air transport of cattle occurred. A plane carrying twenty calves took off headed for a New York. The pilot symbolically followed the Chisholm Trail northward for a short distance after leaving Meacham Field. "Texas Calves Cross Old Chisholm Trail in Plane," *Weekly Live Stock Reporter*, January 2, 1947, p. 1.

30. Only Newark, New Jersey, and Chicago, Illinois, exceeded Meacham as busier airports. See *Research Data*, p. 20714.

31. Blair Justice, "Meacham Field 'Rests' Today After 28 Sparkling and Eventful Years," *Fort Worth Star-Telegram*, April 27, 1953, *Fort Worth Star-Telegram* Clipping File, "Meacham Field" UTA Special Collections.

32. In 1985 the city of Fort Worth renamed Meacham Field "Fort Worth Meacham Airport."

33. "Meacham Airport remains Ft. Worth center of general aviation activity." In 1990 Meacham ranked sixth nationally in take-offs and landings (500,000 plus) because of pilot training.

34. *Research Data*, p. 20716. Also Gouldy, "Pioneer Saw Field Develop From Pasture to Airport."

35. Amon Carter Field or Greater Southwest International Airport closed in 1974 after Dallas-Fort Worth International Airport opened.

36. Collective interview with Butler, Shear, and Cavender. Also interview with Renfro.

37. "Carswell Memorial Park Dedication." Oakwood Cemetery, Fort Worth, March 19, 1993. See also "Major Carswell's Gravesite to be

Moved to Fort Worth Cemetery," *Carswell Sentinel*, December 4, 1992, vol. 34, pp. 1-2.

CHAPTER 9

1. "Sports," *Fort Worth Daily Democrat*, March 11, 1877, in *Research Data*, vol. 33, p. 13147.
2. "Sports," *Fort Worth Star-Telegram*, April 26, 1931, in *Research Data*, vol. 34, p. 13403.
3. "Base Ball Matters: Steps Taken for the Formation of the Texas League," *Austin Daily Statesman*, January 5, 1889, in *Research Data*, vol. 1, p. 396. Also "Sports," *Fort Worth Star-Telegram*, April 26, 1931.
4. Haynes Park was probably not the first. An early baseball park stood south of downtown near the Spring Palace grounds, and another was located in North Fort Worth — which may have been a diamond for a school team, rather than the Texas League. Evidence shows that the latter had to be repaired after the July 1889 flood. See "Sports," *Fort Worth Daily Gazette*. July 9, 1889, in *Research Data*, vol. 34, p. 13242.
5. Interview with Cloud.
6. Flem Hall, *Sports Champions of Fort Worth, Texas, 1868-1968* (Fort Worth: John L. Lewis, Publisher, 1968) p. 64.
7. Sioux Campbell, "Fort Worth Police Band," in *Research Data*, vol. 76, p. 30345.
8. Interview with Bobby Bragan, Arlington, Texas, January 31, 1986. The fact that "Zimmerman" was a German name might have influenced him as well.
9. "Sports," *Fort Worth Star-Telegram*, October 1, 1925, in *Research Data*, vol. 34, p. 13387.
10. Irvin Farman, "Joe Pate Dies At 54, Cat Pitching Great," *Fort Worth Star-Telegram*, December 27, 1948, *Fort Worth Star-Telegram* Clipping File "Pate A-Z," UTA Special Collections. Pate died of a heart attack in Fort Worth in 1948. He was the operator of a downtown news stand and domino parlor.
11. Ibid.; also Frank Tolbert, "We Were All Very Surprised," *Fort Worth Star-Telegram*, January 11, 1940, *Fort Worth Star-Telegram* Clipping File, "Pate A-Z," UTA Special Collections.
12. Art Phelan, "Never Met Anybody Who Disliked Joe Pate — Even on a Rival Team," *Fort Worth Star-Telegram*, December 27, 1948,

Fort Worth Star-Telegram Clipping File, "Pate A-Z," UTA Special Collections.

13. Collective interview, Butler, Shear, and Cavender.

14. Wortham Field, named after Louis J. Wortham, was the Fort Worth Independent School District's playing field before LaGrave Field was built and the school district made arrangements to use it. Wortham Field was located two blocks east of the 600 block of North Main Street. Interview with Rita Renfro, Fort Worth, August 18, 1989.

15. Interview with Bragan.

16. Although the Cats played a game Sunday, they moved the rest of a three-day series to San Antonio. Flem Hall, "Reeves Is Sure Cats Can Meet Home Schedule," *Fort Worth Star-Telegram*, May 16, 1949, *Fort Worth Star-Telegram* Clipping File, "LaGrave Field," UTA Special Collections.

17. Interview with Bragan.

18. After serving as Cats manager, Bragan moved up to the Hollywood Stars, a AAA Pacific Coast League team. He later managed the Pittsburg Pirates in the majors. Fort Worth had remained home for him, however, since his Cats days. He always came back during the off season. Bragan served as president of the Texas League for seven years, 1969-1976, with headquarters in Fort Worth. He served as president of the minor leagues for three years after that in St. Petersburg, Florida. In 1979, Bragan took a job with the Texas Rangers' organization and served as public relations director and director of the speakers' bureau.

19. "Parade Ceremonies To Mark Dedication," *Fort Worth Star Telegram*, July 5, 1950, *Fort Worth Star-Telegram* Clipping File, "LaGrave Field," UTA Special Collections.

20. Flem Hall, *Sports Champions*, p. 69.

21. Collective interview with Butler, Shear, and Cavender. Students on the team in 1912-1913 were Alvin Nugent "Bo" McMillin, Matty Bell, Roscoe Minton, Jim "Red" Weaver, Abe Greines, David Greines, Sol Greines, Sully Montgomery, Bill James, and several others. Hall, *Sports Champions*, p. 66. Sully Montgomery later boxed professionally and then returned to Fort Worth and served as sheriff of Tarrant County in the 1940s.

22. Hall, *Sports Champions*, p. 69.

23. Ibid., p. 66.

24. Ibid., pp. 66-69. Coach Myers resigned the athletic directorship in 1921 and helped his father in business. McMillin went into coaching as a career. In 1945 he coached Indiana to its first Big Ten champi-

onship. He later coached for the Detroit Lions and Philadelphia Eagles.

25. Jim Reeves, "The Buddy System," *Fort Worth Star-Telegram*, June 12, 1988, sect. 5, pp. 1,5.

26. Ibid. Lary returned to Fort Worth after his pro football career and formed a partnership with a longtime North Side friend and former neighbor Bobby Helm to operate a car dealership in Hurst.

27. George Smith, "Neighbors: Elmer Helbing," *Fort Worth Star-Telegram*, September 22, 1980, Scarborough Clipping File. Helbing operated a service station at 604 West Central until three months before his death in October, 1988. "Elmer C. Helbing, 74; raced against Jesse Owens," *Fort Worth Star-Telegram*, October 26, 1988, Scarborough Clipping file.

CHAPTER 10

1. Denton C. Limbaugh, "Racial Elements," *Fort Worth City Guide* in *Research Data*, vol. 47, p. 18415.

2. John H. Burma, "Introduction," to Manuel Gamio, *Mexican Immigration to the United States* (New York: Dover Publications, Inc., 1971), p. vi.

3. "Requiem Mass Set Wednesday For Joe Garcia, Restaurateur," *Fort Worth Star-Telegram*, March 3, 1953, *Fort Worth Star-Telegram*, Clipping File, "Garcia G-L," UTA Special Collections

4. Interview with Esmond Scarborough, Azle, Texas, June 13, 1992.

5. "Requiem Mass," *Fort Worth Star-Telegram*, March 3, 1953.

6. Interview with Scarborough, June 13, 1992. Paul married Hope Garcia. Joe and Jesus had three other daughters; Mary, Josephine, and Pauline.

7. Interview with Lanny and Jody Lancarte, Fort Worth, January 7, 1986. Lanny Lancarte is a grandson of Joe T. Garcia. The present restaurant is located diagonally across the street from the site of the original grocery store at 2140 North Commerce. In later years when Hope Garcia Lancarte ran the restaurant, U. S. Labor Department attorneys sued to force her to set up a $300,000 trust fund for a dozen or so former employees who the Labor Department said were illegal aliens and had been living and working at the restaurant although not listed on payroll records. A lawyer for Ms. Lancarte denied the charges. James Pinkerton, "Joe T. Garcia Suit over back wages," *Fort Worth Star-Telegram*, June 9, 1978, Scarborough Clipping file. The case concluded in 1982 when Ms. Lancarte paid a judgement of

$60,003.59 to the Department of Labor which disbursed it to the employees involved. U.S. District Court, Northern District of Texas, Fort Worth Division, Civil Case 4-76-266.

8. "Pris Dominguez," two-page typewritten fact sheet obtained from Fort Worth Hispanic Chamber of Commerce.

9. Interview with Celia Dominguez, Fort Worth, July 3, 1992.

10. Ibid.

11. "Pris Dominguez" fact sheet. Also John Penn, "P. Dominguez, 65, illustrator and art director," *Fort Worth Star-Telegram*, November 28, 1990, clipping in "Pris Dominguez" File at Fort Worth Hispanic Chamber of Commerce Office.

12. Jon McConal, "North Side Mexican-Americans sought move 'west' of Main," *Fort Worth Star-Telegram*, August 10, 1978 (eve.), Scarborough Clipping File.

13. Ibid.

14. "Diamond Hill League Meets," *Fort Worth Star-Telegram*, August 18, 1940, *Fort Worth Star-Telegram* Clipping File "Diamond Hill," UTA Special Collections.

15. Interview with J. Pete Zepeda, Fort Worth, July 8, 1992.

16. Interview with Hector Beltram, Fort Worth, July 6, 1992.

17. Ibid.

18. Ibid. Laura Beltram died in 1986.

19. Mindel and Habenstein, eds., *Ethnic Families in America*, p. 277.

20. Interview with Michael Ayala, Fort Worth, July 10, 1992.

21. Ibid.

22. Ibid.

23. *Our Celebration*, p. 10.

24. Limbaugh, "Racial Elements," *Fort Worth City Guide* in *Research Data*, vol. 47, p. 18426.

25. *Our Celebration*, pp. 12, 25.

26. Interview with Fr. Leo Delgado, All Saints Catholic Church, Fort Worth, June 7, 1992.

27. The holiday of *el Cinco de Mayo* (May 5) commemorates the 1865 Mexican independence from the French, and *el Diez y Seis de Septiembre* (September 16) celebrates Mexico's independence from Spain in 1822.

28. Interview with Zepeda.

29. Limbaugh, "Racial Elements," p. 18427.

30. Inteview with Zepeda.

31. Interview with Carlos Puente, Fort Worth, July 6, 1992.

32. Indira A. R. Lakshmanan, "R. Mendoza, Sr., longtime civic Hispanic

leader," *Fort Worth Star-Telegram*, June 26, 1992, clipping obtained at Fort Worth Hispanic Chamber of Commerce office. The December 1971 civil action *Arlene Flax v. W. S. Potts #4-4205* E served as the case on which Mendoza filed his later judgment.

33. *The Fort Worth Hispanic Chamber of Commerce 1992 Membership Directory and Buyers' Guide* (North Richland Hills, Texas: Metro Publishing, Inc., 1992), inside front cover. Founding officers of the chamber were Dick Salinas, president; Pete Zepeda, president-elect; Ron Fernandez, vice president; and Manuel Jara, treasurer.

34. Ibid.

35. Ibid., p. 13. The middle schools are E. M. Daggett, J. P. Elder, W. A. Meacham, and Rosemont. Also, interview with Jerome H. Mosman, Executive Director, Fort Worth Hispanic Chamber of Commerce, June 26, 1992.

CHAPTER 11

1. Mrs. Robert R. Truitt, "Pioneer's Rest Cemetery Where the Founders of Fort Worth Sleep," Essay Accompanying Historical Marker Application for Pioneer's Rest Cemetery, May 30, 1978, p. 2. Also Mary Daggett Lake, "Rugged Frontiersmen Buried in Tarrant County Graves Without Identifying Marks," MDL Papers.

2. "Tarrant's Body Is Reburied Here," *Fort Worth Star-Telegram*, March 4, 1928, part 2, sect. 1, p. 1 . See also "County Gives Tarrant Military Funeral Today," Clipping in MDL Papers, Reburial Folder, Series IV, Box 3.

3. Margaret W. Harrison, *The Story of Oakwood Cemetery* (Fort Worth; Oakwood Cemetery Assn., 1970; reprinted, 1980), p. 2.

4. Ibid., p. 1. Also Christopher Evans, "Local History Common Grounds," *Fort Worth Star-Telegram*, October 6, 1991, p. 5, Scarborough Clipping File.

5. Harrison, *The Story of Oakwood Cemetery*, p. 8.

6. Ibid., p. 3.

7. Some other Fort Worth notables buried in Oakwood Cemetery include Winfield Scott, W. T. Waggoner, M. B. Lloyd, Governor Charles A. Culberson, and Elisha Adam Euless. Harrison, *The Story of Oakwood Cemetery*, pp. 5-13.

8. "North Side Development To Be Pushed by Group," *Fort Worth Star-Telegram*, October 16, 1955, *Fort Worth Star-Telegram* Clipping File "North Side Business Association," UTA Special Collections. Board members in 1955 were L. N. Wilemon, Gene

Murray, Dr. Abe Greines, Jeff Christian, D. B. Wiley, DeWitt McKinley, Oliver Shannon, W. O. Freeman, James Bowers, Dr. J. T. Gorczyca, Dick Wallis, Sam Kimmel, Frank Leddy, and Victor White.

9. Jack Douglas, "Pioneer Day Festivities Mark North Side's Welcome to Lights," *Fort Worth Star-Telegram*, April 29, 1956, *Fort Worth Star-Telegram* Clipping File "North Side," UTA Special Collections.

10. Ibid.

11. "Cowtown, U.S.A.," Editorial in *Fort Worth Star-Telegram*, April 25, 1958, *Fort Worth Star-Telegram* Clipping File "North Fort Worth Business Association," UTA Special Collections.

12. "Plan Outlined For Village Of Old West," *Fort Worth Star-Telegram*, September 19, 1958, *Fort Worth Star-Telegram* Clipping File "North Side," UTA Special Collections.

13. Pate, *Livestock Legacy*, p. 276.

14. Ibid.

15. Ibid., pp. 277-78.

16. *Tarrant County Historic Resources Survey*, p. 42.

17. Oliver Knight, *Fort Worth: Outpost on the Trinity*, with an Essay on the Twentieth Century by Cissy Stewart Lale (Fort Worth: Texas Christian University Press, 1990; reprint of 1953 ed.) p. 63. Also *Fort Worth Democrat*, February 22, 1873.

18. Mark S. Leach, "Cowtown Corrals Buys 3.5 Acre Equestrian Center," *Fort Worth Star-Telegram*, "Tarrant Business," July 27-August 2, 1992, p. 18.

19. "It's North Side Today But Oldtimers Recall When It Was 'Marine' and 'North Fort Worth'," *In Old Fort Worth*, p. 93.

20. Interview with Jenkins Garrett, Fort Worth, March 19, 1991.

21. Interview with Esmond Scarborough, Azle, Texas, July 15, 1991.

22. Scarborough, "Reminiscences," p. 87.

23. Ibid., p. 18.

24. Interview with Charlie McCafferty, Fort Worth, November 10, 1979.

25. Interview with Jack Shannon, Fort Worth, March 29, 1991.

Bibliography

PRIMARY SOURCES

Archival Collections

Gary Havard Collection. Fort Worth Stockyards Company Certificates of Stock and Other Records. Fort Worth, Texas.

William E. Jary, Jr. Private Collection. Jary Commission Company and Stockyards Files. Fort Worth, Texas.

Esmond Scarborough. Clipping File and Handwritten Reminiscences. Azle, Texas.

Organizational Collections

C. C. Cummings Collection. *Fort Worth Star-Telegram* Clipping File. University of Texas at Arlington Special Collections. Arlington, Texas.

City Directories, 1927-1991. Fort Worth Public Library.

Corporate Record. 1893-1940. Fort Worth Stockyards Company. Fort Worth, Texas.

Federal Writers' Project. 70 vols. *Research Data.* Fort Worth and Tarrant County, Texas. Fort Worth Public Library.

Fort Worth Hispanic Chamber of Commerce. Brochure, Files. Fort Worth, Texas.

Fort Worth Meacham Airport. Typed History. Fort Worth, Texas.

Fort Worth Stockyards Company Collection. University of North Texas Archives. Denton, Texas.

Local History Collection. Applications for Tarrant County Historical
   Markers. Tarrant County Junior College. Hurst, Texas.
Mary Daggett Lake Collection. Fort Worth Public Library.
North Side Collection. Fort Worth Public Library.
Proceedings of Cattle Raisers Assocation of Texas, 1897. Waggoner
   Library. Texas and Southwestern Cattle Raisers Foundation. Fort
   Worth, Texas.
Sanborn Fire Maps of Fort Worth. (New York: Sanborn Map and
   Publishing Company, Ltd.) University of Texas, Austin.

Unpublished Manuscripts

Dees, Juliet George. "The Clinton Avenue Baptist Church for Slavic
   People: An Emigrant Institution in Fort Worth, Texas, 1920-1961."
   Unpublished research paper for a history course at Texas Christian
   University, 1987.
Hooker, Margaret. "North Side High School and the North Side
   Community." Mimeographed sheets obtained at North Side High
   School, 6 pp. written in 1967.
Lamb, Daniel. "Northside Fort Worth: An Historical Summary."
   Mimeographed pages obtained at North Side High School.
Lamb, Joan. "A Conspectus of Change in the Czechoslovakian
   Settlement of Northside Fort Worth, Texas From 1900 to 1979."
   Unpublished research paper obtained from Czech Community's Sokol
   Hall.
"Orientation to North Fort Worth." Mimeographed Sheet obtained at
   North Side High School.
Ostrako, Lou, "As I Remember," Mimeographed Pamphlet, Fort Worth,
   1990.
Script of Bus Tour Hosted by North Fort Worth Historical Society
   During Chisholm Trail Days, June, 1981. Narrated by Charlie
   McCafferty and Ruby Schmidt.
Untitled story by Johnny Cabluck about his family immigrating to the
   United States and also the Roosevelt Garage. 22 pp. privately printed.
   No date [1988 or 1989].
Woods, Rosemary. "Contemporary Fraternity Within the North Fort
   Worth Czechoslovakian Community and Its Background." 22 pp.
   unpublished research paper for a geography course at North Texas
   State University (now University of North Texas), May, 1978.

Government Records

FAA Southwest Region Recollections and Reflections. A Bicentennial

History Project Prepared and Distributed by the Public Affairs Office (1976).

Niles City, Texas. *Minutes of City Council.* 1911-1923.

North Fort Worth, Texas. *Minutes of Town Council.* 1902-1909.

Office of Secretary of State. Corporations Division. The Fort Worth Packing Company. April 30, 1890. Austin, Texas.

Office of Secretary of State. Corporations Division. Fort Worth Union Stock Yards Company. July 26, 1887. Austin, Texas.

U.S. District Court for Northern District of Texas, Fort Worth Division, Civil Case 4-76-266.

INTERVIEWS

Anderson, Edgar R. Irving, Texas. Typescript of Oral Interview.

Ayala, Michael. Fort Worth, Texas. July 10, 1992.

Beltram, Hector. Fort Worth, Texas. July 6, 1992.

Bragan, Bobby. Arlington, Texas. January 31, 1986.

Brewer, Rex and Lois. Fort Worth, Texas. Cattlemen's Steak House. January 16, 1986.

Butler, Marian. Hurst, Texas. August 18, 1989.

Cavender, J. E. and Ailene. Hurst, Texas. August 18, 1989.

Chester, Opal. Fort Worth, Texas. November 8, 1985.

Cloud, Louise. Fort Worth, Texas. August 20, August 27, 1989.

Cohen, Edwin. Grandson of Meyer and Sarah Greines. Fort Worth, Texas. January 27, 1986.

Cordova, Joe. Fort Worth, Texas. Director, Boys and Girls Clubs of Greater Fort Worth, Texas. June 30, 1992.

Delgado, Fr. Leo. Fort Worth, Texas. All Saints Catholic Church. July 7, 1992.

Dominguez, Celia. Fort Worth, Texas. July 3, 1992.

Dulle, Joe. Fort Worth, Texas. December 30, 1993.

Ellis, Jack and Jackie. Fort Worth, Texas. January 7, 1986.

Franklin, Wilson. Grandson of M. L. Leddy. Fort Worth, Texas. January 8, 1986.

Garrett, Jenkins. Fort Worth, Texas. March 19, 1991.

Harris, Myra. Fort Worth, Texas. City Retirement Office. June 22, 1992.

Jacobson, Hyman. Fort Worth, Texas. December 1, 1986.

Jenkins, Reuben. Fort Worth. August 8, 1989.

Lancarte, Lanny and Jody. Grandson and granddaughter-in-law of Joe T. Garcia. Fort Worth, Texas. January 7, 1986.

Lewis, Alice Marie. Fort Worth, Texas, January 5, 1994.

Moore, Dottie. Fort Worth, Texas. September 24, 1989.

Mosman, Jerome H. Fort Worth,Texas. Executive Director, Fort Worth Hispanic Chamber of Commerce. June 26, 1992.

Murrin, Steve. Fort Worth, Texas. December 29, 1993.

Office Staff, North Side Church of Christ. Fort Worth, Texas. February 5, 1986.

Pappajohn, Mrs. Steve (Georgia). Fort Worth, Texas. August 22, 1992.

Pate, A. M., Jr., Fort Worth, Texas. January 10, 1986.

Puente, Carlos. Fort Worth, Texas. July 6, 1992.

Renfro, Mary. Fort Worth, Texas. November 24, 1986.

Renfro, Rita. Fort Worth, Texas. August 9, 1989; August 18, 1989.

Riley, Bill. Fort Worth Parks and Recreation Department, Fort Worth, Texas, January 4, 1994.

Riscky, Mr. and Mrs. Alex. Fort Worth, Texas, January 5, 1994.

Riscky, Jim. Fort Worth, Texas, December 29, 1993.

Rosen, Ron and Sam. Grandsons of Sam Rosen. Fort Worth, Texas. January 10, 1986.

Samaras, Carnation "Connie" Salicos. Fort Worth, Texas. August 31, 1992.

Scarborough, Esmond. Azle, Texas. July 15, 1991; February 8, May 30, June 13, 1992.

Shannon, Jack. Fort Worth, Texas. January 8, 1986; March 22, 1991; March 29, 1991.

Shear, Dorothy Franklin. Hurst, Texas. August 18, 1989.

Sparto, Mary. Fort Worth, Texas. August 22, 1992.

Strittmatter, Ursula. Fort Worth, Texas. January, 14, 1986.

Wruble, Mrs. Rudolph (Millie Haba). Fort Worth, Texas. July 8, 1992.

Zepeda, J. Pete. Fort Worth, Texas. July 6, 1992; July 8, 1992.

LETTERS

Cabluck, Johnny, to author, December 12, 1989.

ARTICLES

"About the Stockyards Today," *The Fort Worth Daily Live Stock Reporter*, April 30, 1904, p. 1.

"Around the Stock Yards." *The Fort Worth Daily Live Stock Reporter*, March 9, 1903, p. 1.

"At the Big Packing Plants." *The Fort Worth Daily Live Stock Reporter*, March 5, 1903, p. 1.

Baker, Max. "Historic district sought for Grand Avenue area," *Fort Worth Star-Telegram*, January 1, 1988, pp. 21-22.

"Balloon Ascension at Stockyards Inn Park Tomorrow Night By Moonlight," *Fort Worth Telegram*, August 21, 1902, p. 8.

Bartosek, Nancy. "Sokol Celebrates 80 Years," *Lake Worth Saginaw Times-Record*, November 11, 1993.

Brown, Laura Haywood. "Saga of North Fort Worth Baptist Story Community," *North Fort Worth News*, January 22, 1954, p. 10.

"Butchers Go On Strike," *The Fort Worth Daily Live Stock Reporter*, July 12, 1904, p. 1.

Byrne, W. G. "Klan Minstrel Turns 'Em Away; Scores Hit; 'On Again At Church," *Fort Worth Star-Telegram*, November 8, 1924, p. 2.

"Carswell Memorial Park Dedication," Oakwood Cemetery, Fort Worth, Texas, March 19, 1993. (Dedication program in author's files.)

"City and County." *The Fort Worth Daily Live Stock Reporter*, February 7, 1903, p. 1.

"City and County," *The Fort Worth Daily Live Stock Reporter*, February 21, 1903, p. 1.

Dyess, Mary E. "Motivational talents keep the Milan family a winning team with a touch of European flair," *Lake Worth Saginaw Times-Record*, December 19, 1991, p. 10.

"An Electric Railway Ten Miles Long Will Soon Be Built," *The Weekly Gazette*, Fort Worth, Texas, February 1, 1889.

Eyrich, Claire, "So long to an old friend," *Fort Worth Star-Telegram*, February 18, 1980, sect. B, pp. 1,4.

Eyrich, Claire. "Trolleys Clank Gently Into City's Heritage," *Fort Worth Star-Telegram*, August 15, 1965, sect. 2, p. 1.

"Fat Stock Show Begins," *The Fort Worth Daily Live Stock Reporter*, March 5, 1903, p. 1.

"Fire in North Fort Worth," *The Fort Worth Daily Live Stock Reporter*, August 8, 1903, p. 1.

"The Fort Worth Greeks," Clipping obtained from Father John Contoravdis at the Greek Orthodox Church, Fort Worth, Texas.

"Fort Worth's Historical Airport Began in Grassy Cow pastures," *Cowtown Trails* (March 1984): 17.

Gammage, Stefani. "Corraling herds on the street," *Fort Worth Star-Telegram*, May 28, 1992, p. 21 Sect. A.

"Get Down to Business," *The Citizen*, November 20, 1903, p. 1.

Gordon, Jack. "Arkansas Man Tours Texas; Learns Why Cowtown is Different," *Fort Worth Press*, November 17, 1948, p. 16.

"Governor Lanham Can't Come." *The Fort Worth Daily Live Stock Reporter*, February 26, 1903, p. 1.

Haywood, Roy W. "In Old Fort Worth; When the North Side Had only 11 Homes," *The News-Tribune*, July 2, 3, 4, 1976, p. 16. Recollections written in 1927.

"Injunction Sought in Baptist Auditorium Dispute," *Fort Worth Star-Telegram*, November 7, 1924, pp. 1,8.

"It's North Side Today But Oldtimers Recall When It Was `Marine' and `North Fort Worth'," *In Old Fort Worth*, Mack Williams, ed. Fort Worth; *The News Tribune*, 1977, pp. 93-94.

"Justin Ad," *The Fort Worth Daily Live Stock Reporter*, July 27, 1909, p. 3.

Kurkowski-Gillen, Joan. "New Czechoslovakia greets area Sokol gymnists," *Lake Worth Saginaw Times-Record*, August 2, 1990, pp. 1,3.

Leach, Mark S. "Cowtown Corrals buys 3.5 acre equestrian center," *Fort Worth Star-Telegram* "Tarrant Business" July 27-August 2, 1992, p. 18.

"Major Carswell's gravesite to be moved to Fort Worth cemetery," *Carswell Sentinel*, December 4, 1992, pp. 1-2.

"The Marine," *The Fort Worth Daily Live Stock Reporter*, July 5, 1904, p. 1.

Marrs, Jim. "Those who try can find the history of Fort Worth," *Fort Worth Star-Telegram*, undated clipping in files of Nelda Cook.

"Mayor Farmer has a Gavel." *The Fort Worth Daily Live Stock Reporter*, February 11, 1903, p. 1.

McClendon, Mary Helen. "Weatherford Street Home Has Colorful Background," *Fort Worth Star-Telegram*, January 7, 1945, sect. 1, p. 2.

Meacham Airport remains Ft. Worth center of general aviation activity," *Times-Record* Progress 1991 Edition, p. 10.

Monnig's Ad. *The Fort Worth Daily Live Stock Reporter*, February 9, 1903, p. 6.

"Moving Along Quietly," *The Fort Worth Daily Live Stock Reporter*, July 19, 1904, p. 1.

"New Cold Storage Plant," *The Fort Worth Daily Live Stock Reporter*, August 27, 1904, p. 1.

"No Arrests Made in Fire Investigation," *Fort Worth Star-Telegram*, November 7, 1924, p. 8.

"North Fort Worth Council." *The Fort Worth Daily Live Stock Reporter*, February 11, 1903, p. 1.

"North Fort Worth Improvements." *The Fort Worth Daily Live Stock Reporter*, January 28, 1903, p. 1.

"Notes of the Stockyards," *The Fort Worth Daily Live Stock Reporter*, December 20, 1909, p. 1.

"Opening of the Big Plants," *The Fort Worth Daily Live Stock Reporter*, March 4, 1903, p. 1.

"Our Parish at a Glance," Photocopied articled obtained from Father John Contoravdis at the Greek Orthodox Church, Fort Worth, Texas.

Peak, Howard W. "Uncle Jack Durrett, the Village Fiddler," *In Old Fort Worth*, Mack Williams, ed. Fort Worth; *The News-Tribune*, 1977, p. 56.

"Postum Ad." *The Fort Worth Daily Live Stock Reporter*, July 22, 1909, p. 4.

"Probe of Klan Hall Fire Starts," *Fort Worth Star-Telegram*, November 6, 1924, pp. 1, 4.

"Quanah Parker Coming," *The Fort Worth Daily Live Stock Reporter*, March 1, 1904, p. 1.

"Rosen Heights Ad," *The Fort Worth Daily Live Stock Reporter*, June 9, 1903, p. 4.

"Sam Rosen Made a Modest Start, He Now Owns a Fort Worth Suburb," *The Fort Worth Star-Telegram*, October 30, 1904, p. 17.

Selix, Casey. "Still money to be made in building renovations," *Fort Worth Star-Telegram*, June 30, 1987, sect. 3, p. 1.

"Science and Invention Texas As the `Home of Helium,'" *The Literary Digest* (October 11, 1919): 22-24.

Shannon, Oliver. "In Old Fort Worth North Side 75 Years Ago," *In Old Fort Worth*, Mack Williams, ed. Fort Worth: *The News-Tribune*, 1977, pp. 92-93.

Shrake, Bud. "Old Days on Mule Cart Took Madden Through 'Hell's Acre,'" *Fort Worth Press*, September 1, 1957, p. 11.

"Stock Yards Notes." *The Fort Worth Daily Live Stock Reporter*, January 31, 1903, p. 1.

"Stock Yards Notes," *The Fort Worth Daily Live Stock Reporter*, February 2, 1903, p. 5.

"Strike Is Over Here," *The Fort Worth Daily Live Stock Reporter*, July 28, 1904, p. 1.

"Texas Siftings," *Fort Worth Star-Telegram*, December 11, 1988, sect. 3, p. 1. Ad from 1909 *Fort Worth Star-Telegram*.

"To Show in New Barn," *The Fort Worth Daily Live Stock Reporter*, March 3, 1904, p. 1.

Weiner, Hollace. "Packed with memories," *Fort Worth Star-Telegram*, May 14, 1988, part 2, sect. 1, p. 25.

Weiner, Hollace. "Pioneer on the right track," *Fort Worth Star-Telegram*, Sect. B, June 23, 1986, pp. 1-3.

"William G. Cargill Resigns," *The Fort Worth Daily Live Stock Reporter*, October 24, 1910, p. 1.

BOOKS

Bodnar, John. *The Transplanted: A History of Immigrants in Urban Ameria*. Bloomington: Indiana University Press, 1985.

Brown, Lawrence Guy. *Immigration: Cultural Conflicts and Social Adjustment*. New York: Arno Press and *The New York Times*, 1969. Originally printed New York: Longmans, Green and Co. 1933.

The Fort Worth Hispanic Chamber of Commerce 1992 Membership Directory and Buyer's Guide. North Richland Hills, Texas: Metro Publishing, Inc., 1992.

The Fort Worth Police Department. Fort Worth: I. C. Bullard, 1901.

Gamio, Manuel. *Mexican Immigration to the United States*. New York: Dover Publications, Inc., 1971.

Hall, Flem. *Sports Champions of Fort Worth, Texas 1868-1968*. Fort Worth: John L. Lewis Publisher, 1968.

Handlin, Oscar. *Immigration As A Factor in American History*. Englewood Cliffs, New Jersey: Prentice-Hall, Inc., 1959.

Handlin, Oscar. *The Uprooted*. Boston: Little, Brown and Company, 1951; second edition, 1973.

Harrison, Margaret W. *The Story of Oakwood Cemetery*. Fort Worth: Oakwood Cemetery Assn., 1970; reprinted 1980.

Hoffman, Abraham. *Unwanted: Mexican Americans in the Great Depression, Repatriation Measures 1929-1939*. Tucson: University of Arizona Press, 1974.

Joseph, Samuel. *Jewish Immigration to the United States From 1881 to 1910*. New York: Arno Press and *The New York Times*, 1969; originally published in 1914.

Lamb, Ruth S. *Mexican Americans: Sons of the Southwest*. Claremont, California: Ocelot Press, 1970.

Lieberman, Jethro K. *Are Americans Extinct?* New York: Walker & Co., 1968.

Machann, Clinton and James W. Mendl. *Krásná Amerika: A Study of the Texas Czechs, 1851-1939*. Austin: Eakin Press, 1983.

McBeth, Leon. *Victory Through Prayer A History of Rosen Heights Baptist Church 1906-1966*. Fort Worth: Rosen Heights Baptist Church, 1966.

Our Celebration All Saints Catholic Church Fort Worth, Texas. South Hackensack, New Jersey: Custombook, Inc., 1977.

Pate, J'Nell L. *Livestock Legacy: The Fort Worth Stockyards 1887-1987*. College Station: Texas A & M University Press, 1988.

Race, Lila Bunch. *Pioneer Fort Worth, Texas: The Life, Times and Families of South Tarrant County*. Dallas: Taylor Publishing Co., 1976.

Schmidt, Ruby, ed. *Fort Worth and Tarrant County: A Historic Guide*. Fort Worth: Texas Christian University Press, 1984.

Selcer, Richard. *Hell's Half Acre: The Life and Legend of a Red-Light District*. Fort Worth: Texas Christian University Press, 1991.

Servin, Manuel P. *An Awakened Minority: The Mexican Americans*. Beverly Hills, California: Glencoe Press, 1970.

Smith, Sam. *Things I Remember About Early Days In Fort Worth History*. Fort Worth: River Oaks Printing, 1965.

Sowell, Thomas. *Ethnic America A History*. New York: Basic Books, Inc., Publisher, 1981.

Steinfield, Melvin, ed. *Cracks in the Melting Pot: Racism and Discrimination in American History*. Beverly Hills, California: Glencoe Press, 1970.

Stephenson, George M. *A History of American Immigration 1820-1924*. New York: Russell & Russell, Inc., 1964.

Svrcek, Rev. V. A., ed., trans. *A History of the Czech Moravian Catholic Communities of Texas*. Waco: Texian Press, 1974.

Tarrant County Historic Resources Survey. Fort Worth: Historic Preservation Council for Tarrant County, Texas, 1988.

Williams, Mack. *In Old Fort Worth*. Fort Worth: *Tribune* Publishing Co., 1977.

Index

J'Nell Pate, a long-time resident of Fort Worth, is professor of history at Tarrant County Junior College. She received the Ph.D. from the University of North Texas. Mrs. Pate has published extensively, including a regular column "Pages from Western History," for the *Azle News*, as well as scholarly articles and book reviews. Her volume *Livestock Legacy* (Texas A&M University Press) won the Coral H. Tullis award for the best book of Texas history in 1988. That honor is granted by the Texas State Historical Association. Pate is also a fellow of TSHA.